The Oppositional Defiant Disorder Social Survival Guide

ODD Parenting Strategies for Navigating Friendships, Conflicts, and Everyday Interactions

Alex Locklear

Table of content:

Introduction

Understanding ODD and its Impact on Social Interactions

It can be hard to know how to guide a child with Oppositional Defiant Disorder (ODD) through a maze of unexpected turns and changes. You're not alone in this journey, and learning about the unique problems that come with ODD is the first thing that you can do to help your child have good relationships with other people.

ODD is a behavior problem marked by a consistent pattern of being angry, irritable, argumentative, and defiant of adults in charge. It's important to remember that kids with ODD are not "bad" or trying to be hard; their brains are wired differently, which makes it hard for them to control their feelings and read social cues correctly.

Think about it this way: try driving a car that doesn't have works brakes. When the light turns red, the car won't stop no matter how hard you try. In the same way, kids with ODD may find it hard to control their spontaneous actions, even when they really want to behave differently.

This inability to control their emotions can have a big effect on how they deal with other people. They might find it hard to make and keep friends, have a lot of problems with both kids and adults, and have trouble figuring out how to handle everyday things like school, family events, and community   activities.
Kids with ODD often get social cues wrong, which can

cause mistakes and hurt feelings. For example, they might see a joke as an attack on their personhood or a simple request as an unfair demand. Their defiant reactions can then make problems worse and start a cycle of bad interactions.

Another problem they often have is taking other people's points of view. It might be hard for them to understand how their actions affect other people, which makes it hard for them to connect with others and form deep connections.

Remember that ODD is not a flaw in your character; it is a medical disease that needs to be understood, treated with patience, and given the right kind of support. Children with ODD can learn to control their feelings, make friends, and form good relationships with the help of the right tactics and interventions.

Early intervention and consistent, good parenting are two things that research has shown can help kids with ODD do better in life. We can give them the confidence and strength to handle social situations with confidence if we understand why they act the way they do and give them the tools they need to achieve.

These are the things that the ODD Social Survival Guide is meant to give you. We'll talk about the details of ODD, look at methods that have been shown to work for dealing with challenging behaviors, and give you useful advice for making friends and having good times with others.

This guide will help you understand ODD better and give kids the tools they need to do well in their social lives, whether you're a parent, caretaker, teacher, or therapist.

Don't forget that you're not going through this trip by yourself.

An active community of parents, professionals, and groups is ready to offer help and advice. We can help kids with ODD have a better future and reach their full potential if we all work together.

Why social skills are important for healthy growth Having a child with Oppositional Defiant Disorder (ODD) is a big adventure, and we often find ourselves focused on the problems. It's simple to get caught up in the fights, temper tantrums, and what seems like an endless circle of conflict. Even though these things are hard, it's important to keep the bigger picture in mind: our kids are learning, growing, and developing just like any other kid. And social skills are one of the most important things for all kids to learn.

You can think of social skills as the tools we all use to get along with others, solve problems, and do well in our communities. They're what keep us connected with each other, let us share our memories, and help us build a happy life. For kids with ODD, getting better at these skills might be harder, but it's a climb that's well worth making.

Why it's important to be social

Being social isn't just about making friends and being liked. These are basic skills that affect every part of a child's life, from how well they do in school to how happy they are.

A lot of good things happen when you have good social skills, according to research. When kids have good social skills, they often:

Perform better academically: They're better able to collaborate with classmates, follow instructions, and communicate effectively with teachers.

Enjoy stronger mental health: They have higher self-esteem, lower levels of anxiety and depression, and are less likely to engage in risky behaviors.

Build healthier relationships: They form more meaningful friendships, resolve conflicts peacefully, and have better relationships with family members.

Being good with other people can help kids with ODD deal with some of the problems they face. They can help them deal with tough feelings, make it easier for others to understand what they need, and improve their relationships with those around them.

Putting together a base for success

Social skills are like building blocks. These are some of the most important skills kids need to learn:

• Emotional regulation: being able to handle and talk about your feelings in a healthy way.

• Empathy is being able to understand and share someone else's thoughts.

• Communication: Being able to say what you think and feel in a kind and clear way.

• Cooperation is the skill of being able to work with other people to achieve a shared goal.

• Problem-solving: being able to spot problems and settle them without violence.

As parents, it's very important that we help our kids learn these skills. We can show them how to connect with others in a good way, give them chances to practice, and help and support them along the way.

Remember that getting better at social skills is a process, not a goal. Over and over again, things will go well and not so well. But if we are patient, understanding, and give our kids the right help, they can learn to be confident and polite in social situations.

This section is just the start of what we will talk about in this guide when we talk about social skills. We'll talk more about specific tools, techniques, and strategies you can use to help your child become more social. Watch out!

Why kids with ODD often have trouble with other kids

It can be hard for everyone to get along with other people, but it can be especially hard for our kids who have Oppositional Defiant Disorder (ODD). People with ODD often experience heartbreaking times of loneliness, anger, and misunderstandings.

Our whole group has been there. But before we give up, let's remember that the first step toward making things better is to understand "why" these problems are happening.

Children with ODD have a hard time in social situations because of how it describes them. Kids who have short tempers, act defiantly, or have trouble controlling their emotions can get into fights with their peers, teachers, and adults.

It's like trying to play a symphony with instruments that are just a little out of tune. You have to put in a little more work and knowledge to make beautiful music.

Think about a kid named Alex who has ODD. Alex might insist on doing things his way while he and his friends are making a fort, even if it means taking the whole thing apart. His temper tantrums and failure to compromise can make his friends angry and frustrated, which can lead to Alex being kicked out of future playtime. It's easy to blame Alex for his actions, but it's important to remember that his brain is wired differently, which makes it hard for him to get along with other people.

Research shows that kids with ODD often have trouble with social skills like reading social cues, seeing things from other people's points of view, and finding peaceful ways to solve problems. They might not be able to tell when their actions are upsetting or wrong, and they might not know how to say sorry or make things right. Because they aren't socially aware, it can be hard for them to make and keep friends, which can make them feel lonely and alone.

Children with ODD also have trouble controlling their emotions, which can make it hard for them to get along with others. They might get angry, aggressive, or defiant when they are upset or disappointed, which makes it hard for them to do things with others or follow the rules.

This impulsivity can make friends and adults dislike the person, leading to a circle of social rejection and trouble controlling their emotions.

Additionally, kids with ODD might have issues with self-esteem and confidence, which makes it hard for them to make friends or stand up for themselves when they need to. They might think they don't belong or that people don't like them, which makes them withdraw and avoid social settings.

Your first thought might be, "This sounds pretty bad." Is there any chance?" Of course! Children with ODD often have problems with other people, but these problems are not impossible to solve. Let's be patient, understand, and give our kids the right tools to help them get the social skills they need to do well in the real world.

Think about how you teach a kid to ride a bike. They might wobble and fall at first, but with practice and support, they'll finally get it together and fly down the street with poise. To the same extent, kids with ODD can learn how to get along with others, but it takes time, patience, and a lot of love.

In the next few chapters, we'll talk more about the specific social problems that kids with ODD face and look at some good ways to help them get past these problems. We will talk about how to teach social skills, help people control their emotions, boost their self-esteem, and make a safe space for social success.

Remember that the problems our kids with ODD face do not make them who they are. They are smart, strong, and deserve love and respect. We can give them the tools they need to make friends, get past problems, and reach their full potential by helping them understand the "why" behind their social problems.

So, let's go on this journey together, with understanding, kindness, and the firm belief that our kids can do well in the social world.

It can be hard to find your way around the social world, even for adults. When you have a child with Oppositional Defiant Disorder (ODD), it can be hard to handle daily friendships, conflicts, and interactions. It can feel like you're trying to defuse a bomb. Nice to hear that you're not alone. This book will help you find your way through the maze.

This isn't just another parenting book full of vague ideas and words. It's a useful set of strategies and ideas gathered from many years of study, clinical work, and most importantly, the real-life experiences of parents just like you. Not only will it teach you how to live in social situations, it will also help you do well in them.

"How can this book really make a difference?" you may be asking. Well, let's get started and look at how this guide can help you on this trip.

First, we'll simplify the world of social relationships so you can better understand why your child might have trouble in some settings. We'll get to the bottom of why they act the way they do, which will help you see past the surface and react with understanding and empathy. This new way of looking at things can really change things, turning tough times into chances to connect and grow.

The next step is to give you a set of useful tips for dealing with tough social settings. We know how to help you deal with your child's tantrums on the field, handle fights with friends, and teach your child how to make and keep friends.

You can see how these methods work in real life by looking at some examples that were used in real life.

But this book isn't just about how to deal with tough conditions. Giving your child the tools they need to make friends and build good relationships is what it's all about.

We'll talk about ways to teach social cues, build understanding, and settle disagreements without violence. Giving your child these important skills will not only help them get through the present, but it will also set them up for a lifetime of good social interactions.

The part of the book that talks about building your own strength as a parent is one of the most important parts. It can be very hard, both mentally and physically, to be a parent of a child with ODD. We'll talk about ways to deal with your own stress, get help, and enjoy even the smallest wins. Taking care of yourself is very important because you can't pour from an empty cup.

This book is full of true stories from parents who have been through the same thing. Their experiences, both good and bad, teach us a lot and make us feel like we're all in this together. You'll understand that you're not by yourself on this path and that there is hope for a better future.

But this book isn't just a guide; it's an invitation to start a trip that will change your life. It's about changing how you think and how you act so that you can build a stronger, more connected connection with your child. It's about giving your kid the tools they need to handle the social world with poise and confidence.

Then this book is for you. It will help you turn those social problems into chances to grow, give your child the skills they need to do well, and make your family life stronger and happier. We should start this exciting journey together now.

Remember that you're more than just a parent; you're also a teacher, a cheerleader, a guide, and most of all, someone who loves and supports you no matter what.

Chapter 1: Decoding Social Cues: Understanding Non-Verbal Communication (Facial Expressions, Body Language)

You may have heard the phrase "actions speak louder than words." This is especially true for people with ODD when it comes to interacting with other people.

Even though words are important, a lot of what we say is communicated through body language and face expressions. A key skill for managing the social world, making friends, and solving problems well is being able to read and understand these silent signals.

Think of body language as a language that you don't say out loud. If we don't want to say anything, we can show how we feel with a smile, a frown, crossed arms, or moving forward. But people with ODD may have a hard time reading social cues, so this language can be very confusing for them. So, let's go on an exciting adventure to figure out this secret language together.

This will give you and your child the tools to handle social situations with ease and confidence.

Let's start with our faces, which show how we're feeling. A genuine smile can quickly show friendliness and warmth, while a frown could mean disapproval or sadness. Recognizing these emotions in other people can help you understand how they feel and what they want. But keep in mind that facial expressions can be different between people and countries. For example, some people may show more emotion than others, while others may keep their faces bland.

On the other hand, body language is the quiet music our bodies play. Sitting, standing, gesturing, and even the way we look can say a lot about how we feel, what we want, and how we feel about things. For example, open postures with relaxed arms and legs that aren't crossed usually mean that someone is friendly and open, while closed postures with crossed arms and legs might mean that someone is protective or uncomfortable.

It can make a huge difference if you teach your child to read these nonverbal signs. It's like giving them a secret key to figure out how to connect with other people. Just think about how much easier it would be for your child to understand when a teacher likes their work or when a friend is upset. Knowing this can give your child the confidence to act in the right way and make relationships that are better and more meaningful.

However, reading other people's body language is only half the battle. We also need to be aware of our own. We all use body language, and most of the time we're not even aware of it. By paying more attention to our body language, we can make sure that what we do matches what we say, which builds trust and understanding between us.

Practice and study are two good ways to improve your nonverbal communication. Tell your kid to watch people in as many social situations as possible, like the grocery store, the park, and even TV. Question them on what they notice about the way people move and look.

What feelings do they think those people have? What does their body language say about what they want to do?

You can work on it at home with your child too. Play charades with your child. You can act out different feelings or events, and they have to guess what you're trying to say. Or, watch a movie together and talk about what the actors do when they don't say anything. What do their body language and facial reactions say about who they are and how they feel about each other?

Don't forget that understanding nonverbal speech is a process, not a goal. You have to be patient and work for a while. But with your help and direction, your child can learn how to handle social situations with ease and confidence. That can then lead to better ties, stronger friendships, and a stronger sense of being part of the social world.

It's not just a skill to be able to read people's body language; it's a talent. Through empathy, we can connect with others more deeply, understand how they feel, and build trust and understanding. That being said, let's all use this talent to help our kids do well in the social world.

Getting to Know Social Expectations and Norms

Getting along with other people is like a big, complicated dance. There is an unspoken rhythm that everyone follows, which is set by social norms and standards. These are the unwritten rules that help us figure out what's right and wrong and how to act in different situations. It can be especially hard for neurodiverse people to figure out these unwritten rules, like trying to understand a song in a language you don't speak. Don't worry, though! Anyone can feel confident dancing on this social floor if they practice and learn how to do it.

Norms and why they matter

There is something like social glue that holds our relationships together and keeps them from breaking down into chaos. They help us guess what other people will do and say, which makes interacting with them easier and more fun.

It is important to understand and follow these rules if you want to build and keep good relationships. They're not just about fitting in; they're also about getting to know people better.

The Unknown Lessons of Social Interaction

Social norms aren't taught directly like school subjects are. One way to learn them is to watch others, have experience, and sometimes, sadly, make mistakes. The idea of the "hidden curriculum" comes into play here.

There is a hidden curriculum in school that teaches kids how to behave in a classroom. Similarly, there is a hidden curriculum in social life that teaches us how to behave in different chat rooms.

It's kind of like getting better at video games. Most of the time, you don't get a full guide. You learn by playing along with other people, making mistakes, and learning from them. In the same way, we learn social norms by watching how other people act, trying out different behaviors, and changing how we act based on what other people say.

How to Read the Signs: How to Find Social Rules

It can feel like a game of detective work to figure out what social rules are. Look for these hints:

• Look at the crowd: Pay attention to how other people act in a certain place. Are they talking quietly, laughing out loud, or keeping a safe distance?

• Pay attention to clues: Watch how people talk, what kinds of jokes they tell, and how the group as a whole feels.

• Ask people for help: It's okay to ask a friend, family member, or therapist you trust for help learning how society works.

• Make use of your tools: You can learn about social rules from a lot of places, like books, blogs, and even social skills groups.

The Art of Making Changes: Getting used to different social situations

We need to change how we act in different social situations, just like a chameleon changes its color to belong where it is. At a formal dinner party, the rules of behavior will be different from those at a relaxed get-together with friends.

• Look around the room: Pay close attention to how things feel in general. Is it serious or funny? Is it formal or casual?

• Be willing to change: If you find that you're not quite hitting the right note, be ready to change how you act.

• Be yourself: You should be able to change with the times, but don't lose sight of who you really are.

Taking the Journey in

The process of learning social rules never ends. It's okay to get things wrong sometimes. Don't forget that everyone trips and falls sometimes. The important thing is to keep trying and learn from your mistakes. If you're patient, willing to learn, and understand others, you'll become a skilled social dancer who can smoothly move through the complicated world of social interaction.

A Note for Parents and Children

You, as a parent or caretaker, are very important for helping your neurodiverse child learn how to get along with others. Be kind, gentle, and understanding. No matter how small the win may seem, let them know you appreciate it. Don't forget that you're not alone. You can get help with this trip from a lot of different places.

Teaching kids how to deal with social situations

Being able to correctly understand social settings is one of the most basic parts of getting along with other people. It can be hard for kids with ODD to get through this. Their natural tendency to question authority and break the rules can make it hard for them to make good decisions in social situations. However, with gentle help and regular practice, they can learn how to handle these situations better.

Why nonverbal communication is important

Communication that doesn't involve words is very important in social situations. Up to 93% of conversation is thought to be nonverbal. This includes body language, tone of voice, facial expressions, and even personal space. Teaching kids to notice and understand these cues can help them learn a lot about how people interact with each other. A brow furrowed and crossed arms, for instance, could mean anger or frustration, while a smile and an open pose could mean friendliness and ease of contact. Kids can better figure out how other people are feeling by learning to read these signs and change how they act accordingly.

Playing pretend is a great way to learn.

Role-playing is a great way to help kids learn how to act in social situations. By acting out different situations, they can get better at reading body language, responding correctly, and handling possible conflicts. You could make it so that your child is asked to a friend's birthday party, for example. Then you could act out different social situations they might face, like meeting a child on their birthday, playing games, and settling a fight. Your child can gain confidence and learn important social skills by practicing these exchanges in a safe and supportive setting.

Teaching Empathy: Seeing things from Other People's Points of View

Being able to understand and share other people's thoughts is an important part of getting along with others. Developing empathy can be life-changing for kids with ODD who may find it hard to see things from other people's points of view.

Stories are one way to help people understand how others feel. When you read books or watch movies together with people who have to deal with social problems, you can talk about feelings, motivations, and different points of view. Another thing you can do is tell your child to think what other people might be going through and how they might feel.

How Strong Positive Reinforcement Can Be

When you want to motivate and encourage good behavior, positive feedback is a powerful tool. You should praise and celebrate your child's efforts when they correctly understand a social situation or show understanding. This good feedback can help them learn more and feel better about   themselves.
For instance, if your child notices that a friend is sad and offers to calm them, praise their thoughtfulness and

kindness. Or, if they quietly explain their point of view during a fight with a sibling and avoid a fight, praise their communication and problem-solving skills.

Putting together a helpful network

Getting family, friends, and experts to help each other can make a huge difference for kids with ODD. These people can help your child practice their social skills by giving them advice, support, and a safe place to do so. You might want to look for social skills groups or therapy classes that are specifically for kids with ODD.

You can give your child organized chances to learn and practice social skills in a safe place through these programs.

Being patient, persistent, and loving someone no matter what

Remember that teaching kids how to behave in social settings is a process, not a goal. Things will go wrong and problems will come up along the way. But your child can learn to be confident and polite in social situations if you are patient, persistent, and love them no matter what.

Enjoy their wins, learn from their mistakes, and never give up on what they can do. With your constant support, they can get through their problems and do well with other people.

Chapter 2: The Art of Conversation

Starting and Keeping Up Conversations

Talking to other people is what makes social interactions possible. They're what hold our ties together. They're the main way we talk about our feelings, share ideas, and make friends. For neurodiverse people, it can be hard to figure out how to talk to others when they are talking. But keep in mind that talking to people is a skill that can be learned and improved with practice and the right methods.

How to Start a Conversation: The Power of the First Step

Starting a talk can be scary, but it's the most important thing you can do to start building relationships. When you do this, think of it as a friendly request that lets you talk to them. It doesn't have to be big or fancy; a simple "Hello, how are you?" or a word about the place where you both are can work.

Remember that the point is to break the ice and make everyone feel at ease so that they can talk. Genuinely care about the other person, ask them open-ended questions that make them want to talk, and pay attention to what they say. This makes them feel good and shows that you care about what they have to say.

Adding fuel to the fire: keeping the conversations going

The next task is to keep the conversation going once it starts. This is where listening carefully, understanding, and being genuinely interested in other people come in handy.

When you listen carefully, not just to the words but also to the feelings and subtleties that are hidden behind them, you can better understand them and react in a way that helps you connect with them.

Ask more questions, talk about your own situations that are similar, and give thoughtful answers. Don't forget that conversation is a two-way street; both people must participate in order for it to make sense. You can turn a simple exchange into a meaningful talk that strengthens bonds and deepens relationships by taking part and showing real interest.

Overcoming Problems: Getting Past Conversational Obstacles

Neurodivergent people may have trouble starting and keeping talks going in a certain way. Problems can arise if someone has social nervousness, can't read social cues well, or easily gets sidetracked. But these problems can be solved with knowledge and experience.

If you worry about social nervousness, begin with small things. Practice starting talks with people you know in relaxed settings. As you feel more confident, slowly move out of your comfort zone. If it's hard for you to read social cues, pay attention to spoken cues and direct conversation. Do not be afraid to ask for more information or to make your opinions and thoughts known. If it's hard to stay on topic, gently get the talk back on track by asking a related question or summarizing what was said before.

Building bridges: bringing people together through shared interests

Finding things you have in common is one of the best ways to start and keep a talk going. Sharing skills, interests, or experiences can be a great way to start a conversation and make people feel like they belong. You can join clubs or groups that share your interests, go to events that are related to your passions, or just start a talk with someone who is also excited about the same things you are. Sharing hobbies can help people get along right away and give them a lot to talk about.

Accepting Neurodiversity and Celebrating Differences

Don't forget that neurodiversity is a strength, not a problem. Be proud of the way you talk to people and don't be afraid to let your personality show. Being honest and interested in other people are qualities that everyone likes and that can help people bond in meaningful ways.

Take a break if you feel stressed or uncertain. Excuse yourself and think about what you want to do. Remember that being able to talk to people well takes time and practice. Take your time, enjoy your growth, and don't be afraid to ask for help from family, friends, or professionals if you need to.

The Joy of Connection: Getting More Out of Talking to People

Talking to someone is more than just exchanging words; it's a chance to connect, learn, and grow. They make our lives better, help us see things from different angles, and make our relationships stronger. Neurodivergent people can connect with others and enjoy all the benefits that come with it by learning how to talk to people.

To remember, every talk is a chance to grow, learn, and bond. Enjoy the trip, be proud of your unique skills, and don't be shy about reaching out to other people. There are a lot of interesting people and topics to talk about in the world. Just take that first step.

Active listening and taking turns are what make conversation work.

Think of a tennis match: the ball goes back and forth between the players, who are all focused on their turn and ready to receive and react. It can feel a lot like that when we talk, especially with our ODD kids. But we're not trading a soft yellow ball. Instead, we're trading thoughts, feelings, and words. And the flow and pace are very important, just like in tennis.

Taking turns is more than just being polite.

Taking turns isn't just good manners; it's an important social skill that helps people connect and understand each other.

Being able to wait their turn can be hard for our ODD kids who have trouble controlling their impulses or speaking up. Of course, they can learn how to do this with practice and support.

• The Brain Game: Taking turns works out the brain's executive functions, which are the great mental muscles that help you plan, keep yourself in check, and remember things. When our kids practice waiting their turn, these important brain paths get stronger.

In order to increase empathy, you need to wait your turn to speak and then listen to what the other person has to say. This helps our kids understand and value different points of view by building understanding.

• The Respect Builder: Giving someone a chance to speak shows that you value their thoughts and feelings. This is a silent way of saying "I value what you have to say."

Listening to Actively: The Secret Sauce

It would be weird to talk to someone who is looking at their phone or thinking about what to say next. Doesn't feel good, does it? That's why active listening is the key to making a chat interesting.

• More Than Just Hearing: Active listening is more than just hearing the words; it's also about getting what they mean. To do this, you need to pay attention to tone of voice, facial movements, and body language.

The Connection Builder: When we listen carefully, we get to know the person speaking better. They feel like you hear and understand them, which makes the link between you stronger.

The Information Sponge says that paying attention during a talk helps us learn and remember more. We can better understand what someone is saying if we pay attention to what they are saying.

How to Be Successful: Making it Fun and Useful

It can be fun for you and your child to learn how to wait your turn and listen. These are some ways to make it happen:

1.The Talking Stick: This old-school game is a great way to teach kids how to wait their turn. Your child should paint a stick or something else, and the person who has it will get to talk.

2.The Mirror Game: Make funny faces or move around in front of your child. The goal is to copy what the other person does, which helps you concentrate and wait your turn.

3.The Storyteller: Take turns sharing a story. Each person should add one or two sentences. This helps people listen, wait their turn, and think of new ideas.

4.Conversation Recap: Have your child write down what the other person said after you've talked to them. This helps you get better at actively listening.

5.Play a role: Put yourself in different situations, such as buying food at a restaurant or asking for help in a store.

This helps your child get better at waiting their turn and listening actively in real life.

How Important It Is to Practice and Wait

Don't forget that it takes time and practice to learn these skills. You will have to help and encourage your child along the way, but they will learn how to talk to people. Enjoy the process, remember to celebrate small wins, and don't worry about being perfect.

In the big picture, these skills are useful for a lot more than just making friends or managing the playground. Listening carefully and taking turns are important skills for maintaining good relationships, doing well at work, and living a full life. You are giving your child a gift that will last a lifetime by giving them these useful tools.

How to Properly Express Thoughts and Feelings

How to Find Your Voice (and Use It)

The ability to describe ourselves is one of the most basic parts of getting along with other people. Being able to share our ideas, feelings, and points of view with the world is like having a superpower. These things can be hard for our kids with ODD at times. But keep in mind that practice and knowledge are the most important parts of any ability.

How Important It Is to Be Honest

Not only does expressing our thoughts and feelings help us get our point across, it's also good for our health.

When you hold your feelings inside, it's like trying to hold a beach ball underwater—it takes work, and it will finally come up. Sharing our feelings, whether they are happy, angry, or sad, helps us deal with them in a healthy way.

• Building relationships: When we say what we think, we build bridges. It lets others know who we are and what we value, which builds relationships based on respect and understanding.

• Resolving Conflicts: When we disagree, being clear and polite about our feelings is important for finding answers that work for everyone.

The ODD Challenge: How Strong and How Loud It Is

Our kids with ODD often feel things very strongly. They have this as a core part of their neurodiversity.

This level of intensity can be a great source of fire and creativity, but it can also make it hard to control your feelings and say what you want to say.

• The Emotional Rollercoaster: For kids with ODD, their feelings can be too much, which can cause them to act out or hide. It's important to recognize how bad their situation is and help them find healthy ways to deal with their feelings.

• Being Opinionated: Kids with ODD often have strong views that they make up quickly. This can sometimes seem like being stubborn or unwilling to change. They need to learn that it's okay to have strong ideas, but it's also important to respect and listen to other people's points of view.

How to Teach Good Expression

Here are some things you can do to help your child with ODD master this superpower:

• The Feeling Vocabulary: A lot of kids, especially those with ODD, don't have a lot of words for feelings. Help them make it bigger. Instead of "mad," use words like "frustrated," "disappointed," or "annoyed." The more detailed your understanding, the better they'll be able to talk to you.

• The "I" Statement: Tell your kid to use "I" words to talk about how they feel or what they think. By saying "I feel frustrated when..." or "I think...", you move the attention from who is to blame to your own experience, which makes it less heated.

• How to Actively Listen: It goes both ways! Teach your kid to listen to other people and not just wait their turn to talk. This shows respect and helps them see things from other points of view.

• The Calm-Down Corner: Give your child a place they can go to calm down when they are feeling angry or upset. This could be a quiet spot with things to do or senses to help you relax.

• The Power of Role-Play: Act out different situations with a friend. Act like you're arguing or telling someone great news. This gives your child a chance to learn these skills without any stress.

• The Celebration of Success: When your child uses their "expression superpower" well, celebrate! It does a lot of good to give praise.

Don't forget that this is a trip, not a race. Your child can learn to use the power of their voice and become a confident and good communicator with your help, understanding, and regular practice.

Learning about the different ways people talk to each other People who feel like they talk a different language than others, even when they use the same words, are not alone. Hello and welcome to the interesting world of conversation styles! Just like our kids are all different, we all have our own ways of saying what we think and feel. We can make great relationships because of these differences, but if we're not aware of them, they can also lead to misunderstandings.

To have deeper talks and make relationships stronger in the world of neurodiversity, you need to understand these different styles. You feel like you have a secret ring that can help you figure out what someone is trying to say and do. Let's look at the most common ways people talk to each other and learn how to handle them with kindness and understanding.

The Direct Communicator: This person doesn't take the high road and says it like it is. They care most about being honest and getting things done quickly. People who like things to be more gentle may find their honesty pleasant, but others may find it rude or insensitive.

Remember that they generally mean well, even if they could improve the way they say things.

For example, if your child's friend says, "Your cookies taste weird!" it might hurt, but they're just saying what they think. Simply say, "That's an interesting observation. What didn't you like about them?" This will start a conversation and teach them how to speak more politely.

The Indirect Communicator: This person is great at giving behind-the-scenes hints and cues. They might want to avoid open conflict and instead use body language, tone of voice, or even silence to say what they need and how they feel. For those who put in the work to figure them out, the prize is a stronger bond based on trust and knowledge.

If your child says, "I guess I'm not hungry," after turning down dinner, they may be upset about something else. Ask them gently, "Is everything okay? You seem a little down?" This will make them feel free to talk about how they're feeling.

The Thinking Communicator: This type of person loves to think about what they are saying before they speak. It might take them a while to come up with an idea, and their talks can feel like they go into a subject in great depth. Intellectual connections are important to them, and they like people who can follow their train of thought.

When the friend of your child pauses for a long time before addressing a question, don't talk to fill the time. Leave them alone so they can think and talk at their own speed. It's possible that the answer they give will surprise you.

The Feeling Communicator: This person is all about feelings and getting to know other people. They are honest and open when they talk, and they expect others to do the same. The most important things to them are empathy and compassion, and they do best in situations where they can be open and honest.

Case in point: If your child starts crying after a small argument with a friend, don't brush off their feelings. Say something like, "It's okay to be upset. What happened that made you feel this way?" This will help them understand and deal with their feelings in a healthy way.

Remember that these are only a few of the many ways people can talk to each other. Being open to learning, fluid, and able to change is key. By knowing these differences, we can improve how we talk to each other and make the space where everyone feels welcome and supported.

Chapter 3: Making and Keeping Friends: The Importance of Friendship for Children with ODD

How Important It Is to Connect

Friendship is more than just getting together for play dates and sharing jokes. It's a lifesaver, especially for kids who have Oppositional Defiant Disorder (ODD). Because they are often misunderstood and dealing with tough feelings, these kids find safety in friendship, a place where they fit and are loved just the way they are. They can learn, grow, and do well there.

Not Just Games and Fun

For kids with ODD, friendship does a lot more than just make them happy and laugh. It's a place to learn important social skills. They learn how to share, wait their turn, argue, compromise, and settle disagreements by spending time with friends. These are all skills that they sometimes find hard to master. Friendship is where they learn how to give and take in interactions, which helps them become more emotionally intelligent and strong.

A Protection Against Threats

One amazing thing about friendship is that it can keep you safe. Research has shown that kids with ODD who have lots of good friends are less likely to have anxiety, sadness, and other mental health problems. Being friends with someone protects them from the bad effects of stress and hardship. It gives them warmth and support when they need it the most, like a warm hug on a cold day.

Rising Your Self-Esteem

Lots of kids with ODD don't like themselves very much. They might feel different, not good enough, or not worthy. Being friends with someone is a powerful way to fight these thoughts. A child's sense of self-worth goes up when their friends like and accept them. They see themselves through the eyes of others, and they see love, friendship, and kindness. This good feedback helps them feel better about themselves and build a stronger sense of self.

Making people feel like they belong

Every kid wants to fit in. This need is even more important for kids with ODD. They might feel like they don't belong and find it hard to fit in with their friends. They feel like they fit when they have friends because they are a part of something bigger than themselves. Connecting with other people can change their lives by giving them a sense of direction and purpose.

Helping with the growth of social and emotional skills

Making friends isn't just a fun thing to do; it's important for your social and mental growth. A lot of the time, kids with ODD have trouble understanding and controlling their feelings. They learn how to notice and talk about their feelings in healthy ways by spending time with friends. Empathy, the ability to understand and share another person's thoughts, is also something they learn. These skills are very important for having good partnerships all through your life.

Getting Around the World Together

Imagine a child with ODD who has to figure out how to deal with other people on their own. It's like waves moving a ship around without a pilot. But when they have friends, it's like a group of ships moving together. They help each other get through hard times, share information and tools, and stand by each other. You need friends to stay alive, so friendship isn't just for fun.

A Message of Hope

It's impossible to say enough about how important friendship is for kids with ODD. It brings happiness, help, knowledge, progress, and hope. It's a lifeline that helps them get through life's trials and do well. As parents, we have a big part to play in helping these friendships grow. You give your kids a gift that will last a lifetime when you help them make friends.

Remember that every kid should have the chance to feel the magic of friendship. Making friends isn't enough; you need to make a change too.

How to Make Friends: Common Problems

Sometimes it feels like you don't have a plan to help you find your way through the social world. There are many turns and ends that you didn't see coming. Making friends is the same. Going on this journey is full of both exciting prospects and frustrating problems. Your kid isn't the only one having trouble making friends. Many people, whether they are neurodiverse or not, have trouble making friends.

Fear of being turned down is a common problem. This fear can be so strong that it keeps people from even trying to connect with others. They could be afraid of what they'll say, not being interesting enough, or just not being liked. But keep in mind that this fear affects everyone in some way. Putting yourself out there will make you feel that way.

Another problem is social anxiety, which can make interacting with other people very stressful. It could show up as a racing heart, sweaty hands, or a voice that stutters. It can be hard to relax and be yourself when you have these physical signs, which can make it even harder to connect with other people. But there are ways to deal with social anxiety, like practicing awareness, deep breathing, and slowly going into social situations.

Sometimes the problem is that people don't know how to start or keep a chat going. It might be hard to figure out what to say, how to keep the conversation going, or how to politely end a conversation. These are skills that you can learn and use. You can learn these useful skills from a lot of different places, like books, papers, and even social skills groups.

It can be hard to find people who share your hobbies. There's no better way to connect with someone than to talk about something you both like. It can be hard to find those people, though, especially if your child has unusual or niche hobbies. Tell them to find clubs or groups that are connected to what they're interested in and be willing to meet new people there.

There are times when the hardest thing is just getting to meet new people. This is especially important if your child is homeschooled, lives in the country, or doesn't have many social chances for some other reason. In these situations, it's important to make it a point to connect with other people. To do this, you could sign them up for events outside of school, set up play dates, or just tell them to start conversations with people they see every day.

Masking is another problem that a lot of neurodiverse people have. Masking is when they hide or downplay their neurodivergent features to fit in. It may seem like a good idea to mask in order to make friends, but it can fail. Keeping up a front can be tiring, and it can keep people from getting to know the real you. Help your kid find friends who like them just the way they are and embrace what makes them special.

It's also important to keep in mind that not all friendship attempts will work out. People's personalities don't always get along, or their hobbies change over time. If you lose friends, that's okay. It doesn't mean that your child is bad or not worth being friends with. This only means that it didn't fit right. Tell them to think about the good things about the friendship, take what they've learned, and move on.

You have to be patient, work hard, and wait to make friends. Bad things will happen and losses will happen, but there will also be wins and successes.

A good conversation, a shared laugh, or a new link are all small wins that should be celebrated. These small steps can help your child make friends that will last and make their life better.

Remember that everyone has their own path to friendship. You can't use the same method for everyone.

Tell your kid to be themselves, follow their hobbies, and be willing to try new things. They can make real bonds that last a lifetime if they put in the time, effort, and patience.

Teaching people how to get along with others to make friends
Making and having friends is an important part of any child's life, but it can be especially hard for kids with Oppositional Defiant Disorder (ODD). Their strong personalities and trouble controlling their feelings can make it hard for them to get along with their peers. Don't worry, though! Your child can do very well in the world of friends if you help them and teach them specific social skills.

Why it's important to be social

Having good social skills is like having a secret code ring that helps our kids understand and respond to social cues. You need these skills to start talks, understand feelings, settle disagreements, and keep relationships healthy. Getting good at these skills can help kids with ODD feel like they fit and are connected to others.

Children who have good social skills are more likely to have good relationships with their peers, feel good about themselves, and do well in school. They are also less likely to have problems with their mental health, such as worry, depression, and others. So, teaching your child how to get along with others is an investment in their health and happiness.

What Makes Friendship Work

Making friends is a lot like putting together a LEGO wonder. Each brick stands for a different social skill, and when all of them are put together, they make a strong building that will last. These are some important social skills that will help your kid make friends:

1. Starting Conversations: Tell your kid to smile and say "hello" to strangers when they see them. They can also ask questions, share something interesting, or give someone a praise. Always keep in mind that the first step is usually the hardest. But with practice, it gets easier.

2. Active listening: Teach your kid to pay attention, look the other person in the eye, and nod their head to show they are paying attention. You can also ask questions to get more information or show that you are interested in what is being said.

3. Sharing and Taking Turns: Teach your kid why it's important to share and wait their turn. You can practice this through games, hobbies, and the way you talk to people every day. Help them be patient while they wait their turn and share their snacks or toys with other kids.

4. Empathy and Understanding: Help your child recognize and understand the different feelings they and other people have. Teach them to care about other people and to put themselves in other people's shoes. You can read books, talk about different situations, and play pretend to do this.

5. Resolution of Conflicts: Teach your child how to settle disagreements in a polite and calm way. Tell them to be cool when they talk about how they feel, to listen to the other person, and to work together to solve the problem.

How it Works in Real Life

There is no one way to teach social skills that works for everyone. You have to be patient, consistent, and ready to change based on your child's needs. To help you get started, here are some useful tips:

Teenagers and kids learn by watching and copying the people in their lives. Help your kid learn how to treat others with kindness and care.

• Use real-life situations: every exchange is a chance to teach social skills. Show them social cues, let them practice different responses, and give them positive comments.

• Role-playing: Put your kid in different social situations and act them out with them. This will help them practice their social skills in a safe setting. You can do this at home, in therapy, or with a friend or family member you trust.

• Reward successes: When your child learns a new social skill, praise their hard work and celebrate their win. They'll feel better about themselves and want to keep learning because of this.

• Get professional help: If your child is having trouble with social skills, don't be afraid to get help from a professional. A therapist can help and support each person in their own unique way.

Dealing with Problems by Being Patient and Understanding

Remember that getting better at social skills takes work and time. Things will go wrong and problems will come up along the way. But if you are there for them always and are patient and understanding, your child can get past these problems and make real friends.

Honor their growth, no matter how little it is. Pay attention to their skills and push them to do their best. And most importantly, have faith in their ability to make friends and build a social life that makes them happy.

Your child can do well in the world of friends with your help and love.

In conclusion

Teaching people how to make friends through social skills is a process, not a goal. It is a process of learning and growing all the time. By teaching your child about the basics of friendship and giving them useful tips, you can give them the skills they need to feel comfortable in social situations and make friends that will last.

Getting through disagreements and keeping friendships
There will always be disagreements in any relationship, even bonds. For kids and teens who are neurodiverse and may have trouble communicating and getting along with others, these issues can seem even more difficult. With the right knowledge and strategies, though, these problems can be turned into chances to grow and make bonds stronger. Let's talk about how we can give our kids with ODD the tools they need to deal with disagreements and make friends that will last.

How to Understand the ODD Viewpoint on Conflict

It's important to know how kids with ODD might see and respond to conflicts before you start looking for ways to solve them. Because of traits like strong emotional reactions and acting on impulses, they might find it hard to control their feelings when they disagree with someone. This could cause violent outbursts, withdrawal, or even a total shut down. As parents and guardians, the first thing we need to do is recognize these problems and find ways to solve them with understanding and patience.

The Art of Talking to People Well

It's important for couples to talk to each other, especially when there are disagreements. Teaching our kids with ODD how to communicate well can make all the difference.

Encourage them to be honest about how they feel and what worries them. Help them understand how important it is to actively listen, which means they should not only hear what the other person is saying but also try to see things from their point of view. This can be especially hard for kids with ODD who have trouble controlling their impulses and not talking to other people at the right time.

But with constant practice and positive reinforcement, they can learn to have deep conversations that help people understand each other and work out their differences in a friendly way.

A collaborative approach to solving problems

Instead of focusing on who is to blame when there is a fight, tell your child to see it as a problem that they and their friend need to fix together. A fun and interesting way to get them involved in the process is to have them come up with possible answers. Help them think about the pros and cons of each option and come up with an answer that works for everyone. This way of working together not only ends the argument, but it also teaches them useful skills for fixing problems that they can use in other parts of their lives.

How to Teach the Power of Apology

Anyone can find it hard to say sorry, but kids with ODD may have a harder time owning up to their mistakes. But it's an important skill for keeping partnerships healthy. Make sure your kid knows that saying sorry doesn't make them weak; it means they care about their friends and are ready to own up to their mistakes. Make sure they know the difference between an honest explanation and a fake one. An honest explanation recognizes the harm done, admits fault, and promises to make things right. Your child is more likely to follow your lead if they see you acting in this way.

Promoting understanding and taking many points of view

To deal with problems and make relationships stronger, you need to be able to understand and share other people's thoughts. Empathy can take time to develop in kids with ODD because they may have trouble reading social cues and understanding how other people feel. Tell them to try to see things from their friend's point of view and imagine being in their place. This can help them understand their friend's feelings and reasons better, which can help them solve the problem more compassionately and effectively.

This is what parents and caregivers do:

As parents and other adults who care for our ODD children, it is very important that we help them deal with conflicts and keep their friendships. Here are some ideas to help you get there:

• Show kids how to behave; they watch us and learn from

us. Be a good example of how to handle disagreements in your own relationships.

• Make a safe space: Give your child a place where they can talk about their feelings and worries that is safe and supportive.

• Have patience and understand that things take time to change. Thank people for their support and celebrate small wins along the way.

• Get professional help if you need it. If you're having trouble controlling your child's behavior, don't be afraid to talk to an ODD-specialized therapist or psychologist.

By teaching our kids with ODD these important skills and always being there for them, we can give them the tools they need to make friends that last. Even though they are hard, disagreements can lead to better relationships and more emotional growth.

Remember that every disagreement is a chance to grow, and with the right help, our kids can come out of these times stronger, more caring, and better at getting along with others.

Chapter 4: Defiance and Disrespect: Understanding Why Children with ODD Struggle with Authority

One of the most confusing and frustrating things about having a child with oppositional defiant disorder (ODD) is that they may always fight with authority. It looks like every request, rule, and expectation is met with defiance and pushback. But have you ever thought about why? What's going on beneath the surface of this resistance that never seems to end?

Finding Out Where Defiance Comes From

As it turns out, rebellion is more than just disobeying someone; it's a complicated behavior that has deep roots. A lot of the time, kids with ODD have trouble controlling their feelings, reading social cues, and knowing what will happen when they do something. They may see people in charge as scary or controlling, and they may think that rules are made up and not fair.

For a moment, picture yourself trying to find your way through a maze without a plan. Perhaps you're upset, baffled, or even angry. When someone tries to help you, you might get angry, even if they mean well. A child with ODD might feel the same way when they are told what to do or follow the rules. They don't have the emotional and mental tools—the internal map—to handle these scenarios well.

How emotional dysregulation plays a part

One big reason why kids with ODD act defiant is that they have trouble controlling their emotions. This means they have trouble controlling their feelings, especially anger and rage. A child with ODD may act out toward adults in charge as a way to deal with their feelings when they become too strong.

It's like a pressure cooker. It needs a way to let out its pressure when it builds up inside. Defiance can be a way for a child with ODD to let off steam. It's not an excuse for what they did, but it is an important piece of the picture to understand.

What Cognitive Distortions Do to People

Cognitive errors are another important thing to think about. These are bad ways of thinking that can change the way a child sees the world. For example, a child with ODD might think that a parent's rule or a teacher's request is an attack on their person.

These errors can make people more defiant by making them feel wronged and angry. Children are more likely to fight with adults when they think they are being treated badly.

How important it is to connect and understand

It's important to know why your child is defiant, but it's also important to remember that your child is not their disorder. Each person is different, with their own skills and weaknesses and a strong need for love and connection.

When you treat your child with kindness and understanding, you make it safe for them to talk about their feelings and problems. You build trust with them, which can help them get through the maze of power with more strength and confidence.

Tips for Parents on How to Handle Defiance

Okay, so what can you do as a parent to help your kid deal with their problems with authority? Here are some ideas to think about:

1. Encourage Emotional Regulation: Help your child learn healthy ways to deal with stress and anger. This could mean teaching them deep breathing exercises, ways to be more mindful, or doing physical things that help them get rid of stress.

2. Challenge Cognitive Distortions: Gently question the bad ways your child thinks. Help them see things from different points of view and think about how things could be interpreted in different ways.

3. Setting clear goals and consequences is step three. Set clear standards and rules, and make sure they are always followed by giving the right consequences. For a child with ODD, this can be comforting because it gives them a feeling of structure and predictability.

4. Work together with teachers and other adults in charge: Together with your child's teachers and other adults in his or her life, make the setting consistent and helpful. Talk about the problems your child is having and the things that have worked well at home.

5. Get help from a professional: Please don't be afraid to get help from a therapist or counselor who deals in ODD. They can give you useful information and suggestions on how to deal with rebellion and get along well with people in charge.

It takes time to raise a child with ODD; it's not a race. Over and over again, things will go well and not so well. But if you are patient, understanding, and love your child no matter what, you can help them get through hard times and do well in a world that can be confusing and stressful.

Teaching kids how to communicate and work together with respect

With a child who has been identified with Oppositional Defiant Disorder (ODD), going out with other kids can feel like walking through a minefield. Disrespect and defiance can be big problems that cause fights at home, school, and in social situations. You can give your child the tools they need to have healthier relationships and better interactions by showing them how to communicate politely and work together.

Speaking politely is more than just saying "please" and

"thank you." It's about being kind when you say what you need or want, really listening to others, and appreciating different points of view. Cooperation means working together to reach common goals, being willing to give in when needed, and knowing that everyone has a part to play in making things happen. These skills are necessary for getting along with others and being healthy in general.

Ways to Talk to Others with Respect

You can teach your child how to talk to others politely by showing them how to do it yourself. Kids learn by watching and copying what adults do, so be sure that you always treat others with care. Even if you don't agree with their behavior, be polite, listen to what they have to say, and acknowledge how they feel.

Help your kid figure out how they feel and talk about it in a healthy way. Help them tell the difference between how they feel and what they do. It's okay to be mad, but it's not okay to act out your anger by being rude or violent. Help them find words to describe how they feel, like "I'm feeling frustrated" or "I'm feeling hurt."

Active listening is an important part of talking to someone with respect. To show that they are interested and paying attention, teach your child to make eye contact, nod, and ask clarification questions. Restate what they say to show that you understand and care about what they're saying.

Encouragement of Cooperation

Everyone is more likely to work together when they feel heard and valued. Include your child in making choices as much as possible. This could be as easy as letting them pick between two outfits or as hard as working together on chores around the house. Giving them a voice makes them feel like they own what they're saying and gives them power.

Show your kid how to find a middle ground. Tell them that we can't always get what we want, but that everyone can be happy if they can find a middle ground. Play pretend situations that will help you learn how to negotiate and find answers that work for everyone. When disagreements happen, help your child figure out how to solve them. Get them to figure out what the problem is, come up with possible answers, weigh the pros and cons of each choice, and then decide what to do as a group.

This way of working together encourages them to work together and gives them useful skills for dealing with problems in the future.

Being patient and using positive reinforcement

Positive feedback is a strong way to change how people act. When your child behaves well or cooperates, honor their efforts by giving them specific praise. If you're not saying "good job," add "I really appreciate how you used your words to express your feelings" or simply "Thank you for working with me to find a solution that works for both of us."

Don't forget that change takes time. These are skills that your child will not learn quickly. Things will go wrong and problems will come up along the way. If someone is rude or defiant, stay cool and consistent in how you deal with them. Do not fight over who is in charge. Instead of striking, teach and guide.

Spending time and energy showing your child how to communicate politely and work with others is an investment that will pay off for the rest of their lives.

These skills will not only help them get along better with others, but they will also make them healthier and happier in general.

How to Deal with Defiance in Social Situations

To be honest, even the most well-behaved child will act up every once in a while, especially around other kids. This is a normal part of growing up and is usually caused by a need for independence or trouble handling strong feelings. If your child has Oppositional Defiant Disorder (ODD), these defiant actions may happen more often, be more severe, and be harder to handle.

But there is good news: you can do something. You can help your child handle social situations with ease and strength if you know what to do. Remember that your goal isn't to get your child to stop defying you. Instead, you want to teach them how to talk about their feelings and needs in healthy, helpful ways.

Getting ready for the game: the pre-game

It's like a coach getting their team ready for a big game. You can do the same for your child with social settings. Talk to them first about what to expect. Who is going to be there? What kinds of things are going to happen? Giving your child information about what's going on will make them feel better and make them less likely to act out.

Next, come up with a plan. You and your child should agree on clear goals for the relationship. Could be saying "please" and "thank you," or it could be sharing things. Your child will stay inspired and on track if they have clear goals.

The Power of Play: Getting Ready for Real Life

Since kids learn best when they play, why not make the most of it? Your child can work on their social skills in a safe, low-pressure setting by acting out different social situations.

The scene can be about someone cutting in line or a fight over a game. This helps your child learn how to solve problems and gets them ready for problems they will face in real life.

Remember that the point of role-playing isn't to teach your child how to behave, but to give them the confidence they need to handle social settings.

The mid-game huddle: Keeping in touch and staying calm Situations with other people can still go badly, even if you are well-prepared. Your child could get upset, angry, or stressed out. This is when your "mid-game huddle" comes in handy.

First, spend some time with your child. Get down on their level, look them in the eye, and smile at them to make them feel better. Be there for them and let them know you understand how they feel. This easy act of connecting can help calm things down and make your child feel safe.

Next, teach your kid how to use relaxation methods. You can help them get their feelings back under control by telling them to take deep breaths, count to ten, or take a short break. Remember that showing your child how to do these things can be very helpful.

After the game, an analysis: learning and growing together Take some time to think with your child after the social contact is over. Talk about what went well and what could be done better. No matter how small the win may seem, let them know you appreciate it. They may be more likely to keep practicing their social skills if they get good feedback.

Don't give up if things didn't go as planned. Instead, see it as a chance to get better. Talk to your kid about what happened and come up with other options for how they could have handled it. Your child can become more resilient and improve their social skills over time by learning and reflecting on what they have done.

Don't fail to remember the cheerleaders: Putting together a support system

Sometimes it can feel lonely to be a parent of a child with ODD, but know that you're not alone. Talk to your family, friends, professionals, or support groups for help.

Getting in touch with people who understand your problems can give you a lot of support, advice, and motivation.

Remember that dealing with resistance in public is a long process, not a quick one. It takes a lot of love, patience, and determination.

But if you and your child have the right tools and a strong network of support, you can handle social situations with ease and confidence.

Chapter 5: Anger and Outbursts: Recognizing Triggers and Warning Signs

When you have a child with Oppositional Defiant Disorder (ODD), it can be hard to know what to do. Explosive anger, outbursts, and disobedience can happen out of the blue, leaving you feeling stressed and worn out. But if you know what to do and how to do it, you can turn these chaotic times into chances to meet and grow. Learning to spot the specific things that make your child angry when they have ODD is an important part of helping them control their anger. With this knowledge, you can step in early, calm things down, and teach your child better ways to deal with their feelings.

Finding Out What Sets Off Your Child

Each child with ODD has their own set of things that make them angry. These can be outside events, like a change in routine, what you think is unfair, or a job that you find frustrating. They can also be feelings inside of you, like being hungry, tired, or stressed. Pay close attention to the people, places, or things that happen before your child's reactions to figure out what sets them off.

Start by writing down your child's actions in a journal. Make a note of the day, the place, and the exact things or people that make you angry. Find similarities and things that are the same. Did the temper tantrum happen after a fight with a sibling? Was it caused by a change of plans?

With this knowledge, you'll be able to figure out exactly what sets off your child.

Don't forget how powerful open conversation can be. Talk to your kid about being mad. Find out what makes them mad, what they think sets off their rage tantrums, and how they feel before they lose it. This talk can give you important information about your child's thoughts and feelings and help you figure out what sets them off. Keep in mind that cues can change as your child grows and learns. So, make it a habit to regularly review and update what you know about what sets them off. Being aware of this all the time will give you the power to handle situations without losing your cool.

How to Read the Warning Signs

Children with ODD often show small warning signs before they have an outburst, in addition to triggers. These are signs that your anger and frustration are growing. They can be physical, emotional, or behavioral. If you know these signs, you can step in and calm things down before they get out of hand and cause a full-on meltdown.

Clenched hands, fast breathing, a flushed face, or more tension in the muscles are all physical signs. Emotional signs can include being irritable, restless, or moody, or feeling like you have too much to handle. Argumentativeness, defiance, withdrawal, or a sudden change in the amount of action could be signs of behavior problems.

You can also learn a lot from watching your child's body language and facial reactions. An angry face can show up as a furrowed brow, narrowed eyes, or a tense chin. It's important to remember that warning signs can be different for each child, so it's very important to learn your child's specific signs.

Talk to your child about how their body feels when they start to get angry. This will help them learn to recognize their own warning signs. Find out what they notice before they get angry. Being aware of yourself is a very important step in learning how to control yourself. Making a "feelings thermometer" with your child is another idea. They can rate how angry they are on a range from 1 to 10. This visual aid can help them figure out how they're feeling and talk about their thoughts better.

Using Problems to Create Chances

Finding causes and warning signs is not the same thing as controlling your child's behavior. It's about giving them the tools they need to understand and control their feelings. You can give your child a safe place to talk about their thoughts when you notice the warning signs. You can help them come up with ways to deal with their problems, like deep breathing movements, taking a break, or talking about what's bothering them.

Remember that every explosion is a chance to learn and grow. You can help your child learn the skills they need to face the world with confidence and strength by dealing with these problems with kindness, patience, and understanding.

How to Calm Down: Tips for Parents and Kids on How to Get Through the Storm

Anger and outbursts are normal parts of being human, but when they happen a lot and are very strong, they can make daily life hard and put a strain on relationships. These storms of emotions can be especially hard on parents whose kids have Oppositional Defiant Disorder (ODD). But it's important to remember that you're not on this road by yourself and that there are helpful ways to get through these tough times.

How to Calm Down: Strategies for Parents During a Storm

It's easy to get caught up in the chaos when your child's feelings get worse. When you're a parent, though, staying calm is very important for dealing with a problem. As an anchor in the storm, you can help your child find their way back to calmer seas by being there for them.

One strong method is to take big breaths. When our stress chemicals rise, we tend to breathe quickly and shallowly. When you breathe slowly and deeply from your abdomen, your nervous system knows to calm down. Try the "4-7-8" method: take four deep breaths in, hold them for seven, and slowly let them out for eight. Do this several times until your muscles loosen up and your heart rate slows down.

Mindfulness is another good approach. Focusing on the present time without judging it is a way to do this. Pay attention to how your body feels, the sounds around you, and the way your breath feels. Being mindful can help you step back from how strongly you're feeling and reply to your child with more care.

Besides these tips, it's also important to take care of yourself. Spend time doing things that make you happy and calm down, like reading, going for a walk, or working on a hobby. Being well-rested and mentally stable will help you deal with tough situations with your child better.

Finding Your Way Through Calm Waters: Relaxation Techniques for Kids

Kids need tools to deal with their feelings just like adults do. Teaching your child ways to relax gives them the power to control their own emotions and deal with difficult situations better.

One easy but effective method is the "turtle technique." Tell your kid to picture themselves as a turtle going back into its shell. Tell them to curl up in a quiet place and take slow, deep breaths. When they physically pull away, it can help them feel safe and protected while they calm down.

It can also help to picture things. Ask your kid to picture their best spot, like a beach, a forest, or a playground. Get them to give you a detailed account of what they see, hear, and smell in this place. Their minds may be taken to a more peaceful place by this.

Progressive muscle relaxing is another method. This is done by tensing and then calming different groups of muscles in the body. First, do the toes. Next, do the legs, then the stomach, then the arms, now the face. This can help relax you and ease any physical stress.

Making a Peaceful Space: "Building a Calm Oasis"

The place where your child lives and connects with others can have a big effect on their mental health. Making your home a calm and caring place can help lower the number and severity of outbursts. You might want to make a "calm-down corner" in your home. This could be a cozy spot with blankets, pillows, and soothing sensory items like a glitter jar or a weighted lap pad. Tell your child to go to this space when they feel stressed, and give them things that will help them relax, like books, drawing supplies, or a fidget toy.

Make sure your child gets enough sleep and limits computer time before bed. Lack of sleep can make it harder to control your emotions, so it's important to set a regular bedtime routine and make your bedroom a relaxing place to sleep.

Adding mindfulness techniques to the things you do as a family can also be helpful. Someone could do deep breathing exercises with you, everyone could write down something they're grateful for every day in a jar, or you could just sit quietly and focus on your breath for a few minutes.

How to Keep Emotional Bonds Strong: The Power of Connection

In the end, love and relationship are the most powerful ways for both parents and children to calm down. Even if your child is having a rough time emotionally, they are more likely to feel safe and secure when they know you see, hear, and understand them.

You should spend time with your child one-on-one. Do things with them that they enjoy, pay close attention to what they say, and offer words of support and encouragement. Tell them you'll always be there for them. Don't forget that growth takes time and rest. Even though there will be failures, if you keep at it and promise to understand and help your child, you can make your home a better place for everyone that lives there.

In conclusion

Outbursts and anger are normal parts of life. But with the right tools and methods, you and your child can learn to handle these rough waters with more ease and strength. You can create a sense of calm and connection for your whole family by putting your own health first, teaching your child ways to calm down, making your home peaceful, and developing emotional bonds.

Putting together a "Calm-Down Kit" for social situations It's no secret that social settings can feel like a minefield at times. Things that happen out of the blue can set off ODD triggers in anyone, and before we know it, we're angry or frustrated all over again. That's why it's important to have a "calm-down kit"—a personalized collection of tools and strategies that can help us calm down and handle social settings with poise and strength.

Think about having a secret tool you can use when you feel like you can't handle things anymore. Your "calm-down kit" could be a group of tools that help you control your feelings and deal with tough situations in a way that is in line with your values and goals. But what should you put in this kit exactly?

To begin, it's important to remember that everyone is different and what works for one person might not work for someone else. It's important to try different things until you find what works for you. But many calm-down kits come with tried-and-true ways to help people relax.

Deep breathing routines are a common way to help. When we're upset or angry, our breathing tends to get short and quick. We can turn on the parasympathetic nervous system, which helps us relax and feel calm, by actively slowing down and deepening our breath. You can try different ways to breathe, like box breathing or breathing through your opposite nostrils. Choose the one that feels good to you and do it often so you can quickly use it when you need to.

Sense grounding is another useful tool. This means using your senses to bring you back to the present and take your mind off of your feelings that are getting too strong. You could carry a small, interesting-feeling thing with you that you can touch and concentrate on, like a smooth stone or a soft piece of fabric. You could also smell a relaxing essential oil or listen to music or outdoor sounds that are relaxing. Try out different physical experiences to find the ones that help you feel grounded the most.

Another great way to calm down is to use visualization.

Close your eyes and picture a peaceful scene, like a beach or a forest, when you feel frustration or anger rising up. Use all of your senses to picture this: feel the sun's warmth on your face, listen to the waves, and smell the salty air. Better at taking you to a calm state, the more vivid your image needs to be.

Another useful thing to have in your calm-down kit is affirmations. You can say these positive things to yourself out loud or in your head to fight negative thoughts and strengthen your positive views. You could tell yourself things like, "I am calm and in charge" or "I can handle this with grace and ease." Pick mantras that speak to you, and say them to yourself often to really understand what they mean.

Along with these tactics, you might also find it helpful to have some physical activities on hand. Working out naturally lowers stress and can help get rid of anger and frustration. If you feel like you have too much to handle, take a quick walk, do some jumping jacks, or do any other type of exercise that you enjoy.

It's also helpful to have a plan for when you're with other people and something makes you angry or frustrated. One way to do this is to come up with a ready-made line to get out of a situation, like "I need a moment to gather my thoughts" or "I'm going to go outside for some fresh air." Having a trusted family member or friend you can call or text for help could also be part of it.

Don't forget that making a calm-down kit is an ongoing process. There isn't a single answer that works for everyone. Instead, you need to find what works best for you and make your kit fit your wants and preferences. Do not rush your healing, try different approaches, and don't be embarrassed to talk to a doctor or counselor if you require extra help.

By taking the time to make your own "calm-down kit," you give yourself the tools you need to handle social situations with strength and confidence. You are making choices about how to handle problems that are in line with your values and goals and taking charge of your feelings.

Make your own "calm-down kit"—it might be the secret weapon that changes the way you connect with other people and gives you the power to live a happier, more fulfilling life.

Chapter 6: Difficulty with Sharing and Taking Turns: Understanding the Underlying Reasons for These Challenges

Sometimes it's hard to watch kids struggle with things like sharing their toys or waiting their turn in a game without getting upset or worried. But before you jump to conclusions, it's important to understand that these actions aren't just selfish or defiant. Instead, they are usually caused by a lot of different developmental, brain, and environmental factors working together.

Figuring out these deeper causes is the first thing that needs to be done to provide good help and guidance.

What Makes Up the Building Blocks of Social Skills?

Kids don't naturally know how to share or wait their turn. As kids get older and grow, they slowly learn these skills. At different ages, they reach important stages.

For example, children are mostly concerned with their own wants and needs, which makes it hard for them to understand the idea of sharing.

Kids start to understand the value of sharing and cooperating when they start preschool, but they may still have trouble controlling their emotions and impulses, which can make it hard for them to wait their turn.

A child's ability to share and wait their turn can also be affected by their brain. Researchers think that kids with

Oppositional Defiant Disorder (ODD) might have changes in the parts of their brain that control their impulses, emotions, and social skills. While this doesn't mean that kids with ODD can't learn these skills, it does show how important it is to give them specialized help and understanding.

Things in the environment: the part of family and social setting

The family and social surroundings of a child can have a big effect on how well they learn to get along with others. For example, kids who don't get enough social contact or whose parents don't discipline them consistently may have trouble sharing and waiting their turn. On the other hand, kids who grow up in caring places that stress teamwork and understanding are more likely to have good social skills.

There are also cultural standards and norms that can come into play. Sharing is valued and encouraged from a young age in some societies, while competition and individual success may be more important in others. Knowing about these cultural differences can help us understand and deal with kids' behavior in a more complex way.

How to Handle the Ups and Downs of Social Interaction Based on Your Feelings

Kids can feel strong emotions when they have to share and wait their turn. Young children may find it hard to control their strong feelings when they want to play with a toy they really want or when they have to wait their turn. When these feelings get too much for kids, they might act out, refuse to share, or have trouble following the rules.

Understanding how kids' actions are caused by their feelings can help us treat them with kindness and understanding. We can make a safe and supportive space for kids to learn about social relationships by recognizing their feelings and teaching them healthy ways to talk about and deal with them.

Talking to each other and understanding other points of view are important for getting along with others.

To get along with other people, you need to be able to communicate clearly and understand their points of view. Kids who have trouble with these skills might find it hard to understand what other people want and feel, which could lead to arguments and misunderstandings.

We can promote empathy and teamwork by encouraging open conversation and teaching kids to see things from other people's points of view. Simple things that can help with this are asking kids how they'd feel if someone took their toy without asking or having them act out different social situations.

The Power of Positive Reinforcement: Enjoying Little Wins

Children's behavior can be changed a lot with positive encouragement. People are more likely to keep practicing these skills if we praise their efforts and wins. We don't have to scold or punish them for making mistakes. Instead, we can offer support and advice, which will help them learn from their mistakes. Share and wait your turn are difficult skills that need time and practice to get good at. We can give our kids the tools they need to build strong social skills that will serve them well throughout their lives by helping them understand why they are having these problems and giving them patient, helpful advice.

Remember that every child is different, and so will be the way they learn how to get along with others. Honor their progress, accept who they are, and most importantly, never stop believing in their ability to do well in social settings.

How to Teach Sharing and Waiting Your Turn

Sharing and waiting their turn isn't just good manners; it's also a way to teach them important life skills that will help them make friends, solve problems, and do well in social situations. For kids with Oppositional Defiant Disorder (ODD), learning these skills might take a little longer and special plans, but the benefits are huge.

Understanding Why People Share and Take Turns

Let's take a moment to think about why sharing and waiting your turn are so important before we get into tactics. These skills help people work together, care about others, and value them. They teach kids how to get along with others, settle arguments quietly, and understand what is fair. When our kids learn how to share and wait their turn, they gain important skills that help them handle their social lives with ease and confidence.

Getting things ready: laying the groundwork for understanding

For kids with ODD, it's important to make sure they fully understand things before moving on to specific techniques. First, use easy language to help your child understand what it means to share and wait their turn. Use examples from your own life, like how you and your family share toys or take turns picking out a game to play. Stress the good things that happen when you share and wait your turn, like having more fun with friends, avoiding fights, and making your relationships better.

Modeling: Setting a good example

Kids learn from watching the people in their lives. As parents, we can show our kids how to share and wait our turn by the way we act every day. Show your child how you share your time, attention, and things with other people. Show that you can wait your turn in conversations, actions, and making decisions. Your child will understand how important these behaviors are better and be more likely to copy them if they see you do them.

Having fun: games and things to do

It should be fun to learn, especially for kids with ODD who might not respond well to traditional ways of teaching. Include games and tasks in your child's daily routine that teach them to share and wait their turn. Play board games where everyone has to wait their turn and do cooperative tasks where everyone has to share. Give your child chances to practice these skills in a fun, low-pressure setting. Don't forget to praise your child for their accomplishments, no matter how small. This can really help them stay motivated.

Breaking It Down: How to Do It Step by Step

Breaking up hard jobs into smaller, easier-to-handle steps can make a huge difference for kids with ODD. To teach kids how to share and wait their turn, start with simple situations with short wait times and everyday things. As your child gets better, slowly make the puzzle more difficult. Give your child clear directions and visual aids, like a timer or a visual schedule, to help them understand what you want them to do and prepare for changes.

Getting through Problems: Dealing with Resistance and Conflict

When learning to share and wait their turn, kids with ODD may resist or fight. It's important to stay cool and patient, because losing your temper can make things worse. Support your child's feelings while still being strong about rules like sharing and waiting your turn. You can help your child come up with peaceful ways to solve problems by suggesting different options, like agreeing or switching toys. Remember that being consistent is important, so follow the rules in a fair and consistent way.

Celebrating Success: Seeing and encouraging good behavior

Positive feedback is a great way to change behavior, and it works especially well with kids who have ODD. Let your child know you notice when they share or wait their turn, and celebrate their success. Say something like, "I'm so proud of how you shared your toys with your friend" or "You waited your turn to play the game so well." You can encourage your child to keep learning these useful skills by noticing and rewarding good behavior.

Looking for Help: Working Together with Experts

If you're having trouble teaching your child how to share and wait their turn, don't be afraid to get help from a professional. A therapist or counselor who specializes in ODD can help your child by giving them advice and techniques that are specifically designed for their needs and problems. They can also help you make a behavior plan for your child that covers all areas of his or her social growth. Don't forget that you're not going through this alone and that there are tools out there to help you and your child succeed.

Playing games and doing activities to work on these skills

Remember how we said that being able to share and wait your turn are important social skills? Let's get to the fun part: making practice time into playtime! We're going to talk about how games and activities can help your child turn these problems into fun adventures.

Why Play Games? How Playful Learning Can Help You Learn

Playing games isn't just for fun (though that's great!). What great ways to learn and grow they are. Your child can learn to share and wait their turn in a safe, low-stress way through games. It's like practicing how to talk to people in real life, where it's okay to make mistakes and laughing is the best medicine.

Let's play! Things to do that make sharing superpowers

Let's start this fun trip with some games that are great for sharing:

Setting up a "trading post" with your child's toys is called "The Trading Post." Get them to trade things with you or their brothers. This helps them learn that sharing doesn't mean losing something forever and also teaches them the idea of exchange.

It's time to share snacks. Get a plate ready with snacks and ask your child to share them with you or a friend. It can be even more fun if you let them pick the snacks or hold a "snack sharing ceremony."

Three. Cooperative Board Games: Pick board games where everyone has to work together to win. These games teach people how to work together, agree, and know that sharing is good for everyone.

Building Blocks Extravaganza: Get your building blocks out and work with your kids to make a beauty. Tell them to share the blocks, take turns adding pieces, and even help each other out when they get stuck.

Make believe picnics: Spread out a blanket, pack some make believe food, and ask your child to a make believe picnic. Sharing the made-up treats, taking turns being the host, and making choices as a group can all teach you something.

Taking Turns? Let's have a party!

With the right games, taking turns can be just as much fun as giving turns:

Musical Chairs with a Twist: When the music stops, have everyone sit down together instead of going out. This encourages people to work together and let everyone have a chance.

Storytelling Relay: Begin a story, and then have your child pick it up and add their own twist to it. Take turns making up the story and see where your ideas take you.

Lots of card games: Games like "Go Fish" and "Crazy Eights" naturally require you to take turns, which makes them great for practicing this skill.

Dance Party Playlists: Make a mix with other people and select songs to dance to one at a time. You can learn to be patient and enjoy each other's music tastes at the same time.

Outdoor Adventures: Playing tag, taking turns on the swings, or visiting a new park are all fun things to do outside that can be done in groups.

Advice on How to Use Games to Grow Your Business

As you go on these fun trips, remember these things:
• Have patience and understand. Remember that it takes time and practice to learn new things.

• Give praise and support. Focus on the progress your child is making and celebrate even small wins.

• Stay happy and have fun. Allow lots of laughter to happen because the goal is to make sharing and waiting your turn fun.

• Change the tasks based on what your child likes. Pick games and activities that they like and are interesting to them.

• Have fun with it! As you play with your child, show them how to behave and enjoy the time together.

Remember that learning how to share and wait your turn is a constant process. But when you play, you can turn problems into chances to learn and grow, and along the way, you can make experiences that will last a lifetime.

Chapter 7: Bullying and Victimization: Identifying the signs of bullying (both as a bully and victim)

Bullying is a complicated problem that can leave long-lasting scars on both the people who are bullied and the people who do the bullying. It's important for parents and other adults who care for kids to know how to spot the signs of bullying, whether their child is being bullied or is being bullied. We can better help our kids and help them have healthy relationships with others if we understand how this works on a deeper level.

How to tell if someone is being bullied

It's heartbreaking to find out that your child is being bullied, but you need to stay cool and help them. Here are some common signs that you should be careful:

• Changes in the body: injuries that can't be explained, damaged items, or a lot of headaches or stomachaches can be warning signs. Even though these signs don't always mean that someone is being bullied, it's important to look into it further if they happen often.

• Changes in emotions: kids who are bullied might shut down, get nervous, or feel sad. They may also have rapid changes in mood or trouble sleeping. Watch out for big changes in your child's mental health, as these could be signs of deeper problems.

• Changes in behavior: Suddenly not wanting to go to school, doing poorly in school, or losing interest in things they used to enjoy can be signs that something is wrong. Also, keep an eye on any changes in the kids your child hangs out with.

Talk to the other kids if you think your child is being bullied. Help them feel safe by letting them know you'll listen and not judge them as they talk about their problems.

How to tell if someone is bullying others

It can be just as upsetting to find out that your child is bullying other kids. Even though you shouldn't panic, you should talk to your child about their behavior and help them understand how their actions result in things. Keep an eye out for these signs:

• Aggression: Kids who pick on other kids often tend to be physically and mentally aggressive. They could get into fights a lot, say mean things, or scare their friends.

• Putting the blame on other people: Bullies rarely own up to their mistakes. Instead, they often put the blame on other people for their problems or downplay the effects of their actions.

• Lack of empathy: Kids who pick on others often have trouble understanding or caring about how other people feel. They might act like they don't care about the pain they cause, or they might even enjoy it.

• Social manipulation: Bullies may use their social status to control or trick other people. To keep their power, they might join groups, leave out some friends, or spread rumors.

If these things happen to your child, you should talk to them about it in a calm and honest way. Help them see how their actions affect others, and stress how important it is to be kind and understanding.

Why early action is important

Getting involved with your child as soon as possible is very important, whether they are being bullied or are the bully. The sooner you deal with the problem, the more likely it is that you can avoid long-term problems. Early intervention can help kids who are being bullied learn how to deal with it, become more resilient, and win back their confidence.

It can also stop mental health problems like worry, depression, and post-traumatic stress disorder (PTSD) from happening.

Kids who pick on others can learn how their actions affect others, develop empathy, and find better ways to connect with their peers if they get help early on. It can also keep them from acting aggressively over and over again, which could cause problems later on.

Getting your child help

No matter what your child did to cause the bullying, it's important to love and support them no matter what. Make sure they know you're there for them and give them a safe place to talk about how they feel. If you think you need it, talk to a doctor or counselor who specializes in bullying.

Don't forget that the person being bullied is never to blame. There are no easy answers to this problem, but with your help, your child can get through it and do well.

Teaching people how to be assertive and speak up for themselves
Oppositional Defiant Disorder (ODD) makes it hard for kids to get along with others because they have trouble controlling their feelings and acting on impulse. In turn, this can make them more likely to be bullied or hurt. Dealing with bullying directly is important, but teaching your child how to speak up for themselves and express their needs in a strong way is also very important. This proactive method gives them the confidence and strength to handle social situations well.

How to Be Assertive and Stand Up for Yourself

Being assertive means being able to say what you think, feel, and need in a clear, polite, and sure way. It's about standing up for yourself without getting angry or giving up. When someone speaks up for their own rights, interests, or wants, this is called self-advocacy. These skills can make a huge difference for kids with ODD.

• Lessening of Victimization: Bullies are less likely to pick on assertive kids because they show confidence and don't put up with being picked on.

• Better Relationships: Being able to talk to adults and friends clearly leads to better relationships.

• Higher Self-Esteem: Being able to speak up for yourself effectively boosts your sense of self-worth and confidence.

• More independence: Kids who can say what they need are better able to handle different social situations on their own.

How to Teach Being Assertive: A Step-by-Step Guide

How to Define Assertiveness: Help your kid understand that being confident doesn't mean being mean or bossy, it means being honest about what they want and how they feel in a respectful way. To show the difference between assertive, passive, and aggressive reactions, use examples from everyday life.

Role-playing games: practice being aggressive in everyday social situations. You could act out how to say "no" to group pressure, ask a teacher for help, or tell a friend you don't agree with them.

Use "I" Statements: Tell your kid to talk about how they feel and what they need by using "I" statements. They could say something like, "That hurts me when you say that" instead of "You're being mean."

Teach Nonverbal Communication: Being assertive is more than just what you say. Help your child get better at making eye contact, speaking with confidence, and moving their bodies in an open way.

Positive reinforcement: When your child tries to be bold, even if it doesn't work out right at first, praise them. No matter how small, celebrate their wins.

Encouragement of Self-Advocacy

1. Figure out your needs and goals. Help your child figure out what they want and need in different scenarios. Some questions that could help with this are "What do you want to happen?" and "What do you need to feel comfortable?"

2. Come up with answers: Come up with possible solutions to problems as a group. Help your kid see things from different points of view and come up with creative answers.

3. Learn How to Ask for Help: Show your kid that it's okay to ask for help when they need it. For example, you could ask a teacher to explain something, a friend for help, or a trusted adult for advice.

4. Make people think about themselves: Talk about what went well and what could be done better after social encounters. This helps your child figure out what they're good at and what they need to work on.

5. Reward Successes: Recognize your child's efforts to speak up for themselves, even if the result wasn't what you

wanted. Think about how far they've come and what they've learned.

Some extra tips

Take it easy at first. Practice being assertive and speaking up for yourself in low-stakes situations before going on to more difficult ones.

• Be an example of assertiveness. Kids learn by watching their parents. Show that you can communicate assertively with others.

• Get Professional Help: If your child still has trouble being assertive or speaking up for themselves despite your best efforts, you might want to talk to an ODD-specific therapist or psychologist.

Self-advocacy and being outspoken are skills that are taught over and over again. You need to be patient, consistent, and give them good feedback. Don't forget that your child can learn these skills and do well in social settings. You are setting them up for success for life by giving them the tools to speak clearly and stand up for themselves.

Keeping kids safe from bullies and helping them deal with it

Being bullied is a tough problem that can hurt a child's mental health and social growth for a long time. As parents, we want to protect our kids from harm, but it's also important to give them the tools they need to deal with problems and get through them. Within this part, we will talk about proactive ways to keep kids safe from bullying and build their resilience to handle such situations.

Prevention as the First Line of Defense: Building a Strong Base

When it comes to bullying, the saying "prevention is better than cure" is especially true. Even though we can't completely get rid of the risk, there are many things we can do to make the setting less likely to be bullied.

1. Encourage Open Communication: Make sure everyone in your family trusts each other and can talk to each other freely. Tell your child that they can talk about their experiences, good and bad, without worrying about being judged or ignored. As they talk, pay close attention, acknowledge their feelings, and reassure them that you're there to help.

2. Develop Kindness and Empathy: From a young age, teach your child how important it is to be kind and have empathy. Help them learn how what they say and do can affect other people. Tell them to be kind to everyone, no matter how they are different.

3. Give Your Child Power: Teach your child how to be forceful. Put them in situations where they have to stand up for themselves and others. Tell them to speak up if they see someone being bullied and to get help from an adult they trust if they need it.

4. Encourage Good Self-Esteem: Help your kid feel good about himself or herself. Pay attention to their skills and what they've already done well, and praise and support them for it. Kids who have high self-esteem are less likely to be picked on by bullies.

5. back and encourage healthy friendships: Help your child make friends who respect and back each other. Friendships can be a very important defense against the bad effects of bullying.

When there is bullying: How to Help Your Child Get Through the Storm

Bullying can still happen, no matter how hard we try. It's very important to show your child kindness, understanding, and take action if they are being bullied.

1. Listen and make sure: Tell your child that you understand how they feel and that you believe them. Don't downplay their feelings or blame them for what happened.

2. Give your child comfort: Tell your child that you care about them and that they are not alone. Say that it's not their fault that they are being picked on.

3. Write down the Bullying: Keep a full record of the bullying events, including the dates, times, places, and names of anyone who saw it. This information might come

in handy if you need to tell someone at school or another authority about the teasing.

4. Ask the School to Help: Work with the school to stop the teasing. Most schools have rules against bullying, and staff should be taught how to handle reports of abuse.

5. Get Professional Help: If the bullying is bad or keeps happening, you might want to see a therapist or counselor for help. A mental health worker can give your child extra help and teach them how to deal with things.

Your Child Can Cope and Get Better

Bullying can leave deep mental scars that last for a long time after the attack stops. Giving your child ongoing support is very important to help them get better and regain their confidence.

1. Encourage Open Communication: Keep making it easy for you and your child to talk to each other. Make them feel like you'll listen and help them whenever they need it.

2. Build Resilience: Teach your child how to deal with stress and solve problems to help them become more resilient. Help them deal with stress in a healthy way by doing things like working out, spending time in nature, or being creative.

3. Join support groups: If your child has been bullied, you might want to join a group for kids who have been bullied. Support groups can be a safe place for kids to talk about

their problems, make friends with people who understand, and learn new ways to deal with things. 4. Encourage constructive activities: Tell your kid to do things they love. Positive tasks can help them feel better about themselves and give them a sense of accomplishment.

How to Heal and Empower Yourself

It takes a lot of work to keep kids safe from bullying and help them deal with it. It takes a mix of proactive ways to stop bullying, helpful responses when it does happen, and ongoing work to help people get stronger and heal. Don't forget that you're not on this trip by yourself. There are many tools out there that can help you and your child deal with the problems that bullying can cause. You can give your child the tools they need to deal with problems and come out better and more resilient if you work together.

Chapter 8: Creating a Supportive Home Environment: Promoting Positive Communication and Problem-Solving

A good relationship depends on being able to talk to each other and work out problems. This is especially true for families raising a child with Oppositional Defiant Disorder (ODD). These skills aren't easy for everyone, but they can be especially hard for kids with ODD, who may have trouble controlling their emotions and acting on impulse. That being said, parents can give their kids the tools they need to handle social situations and disagreements well by creating a loving home where talking things out and solving problems are valued.

The Power of Words: Communicating in a Positive Way

Our children learn about the world and their place in it through the way we talk to them. Being mean, critical, and negative can hurt a child's self-esteem and make the home life tense. On the other hand, good communication builds trust, improves relationships, and gives kids a safe place to say what they want.

Engaging in active listening is a good way to encourage good conversation. To do this, you need to give your child your full attention, look them in the eyes, and repeat what they say. You could say, "It sounds like you had a really tough time today," instead of ignoring your child's comments about a bad day at school. If you want to talk about it, I'm here to listen.

Positive feedback is yet another very useful tool. When your child speaks well, encourage them and let them know you appreciate it. This could be as easy as saying, "Thank you for telling me how you feel" or "Thank you for making that so clear." You can get your child to repeat good actions by pointing them out.

Solving problems: Changing problems into chances You need to be able to solve problems in order to get through life's difficulties. Children with ODD often have trouble fixing problems because they act on impulse and can't control their anger. But with their parents' help and patience, they can learn how to deal with problems in a calm and helpful way.

The collaborative problem-solving technique is a good way to teach people how to solve problems. With this plan, you and your child will work together to figure out the problem, come up with possible solutions, weigh the pros and cons of each choice, and decide on the best course of action. Staying cool and supportive is important during this process, even if your child gets angry or refuses to do what you want.

Playing a role is another useful method. This means playing out different situations with your child, like how to deal with a fight with a friend or how to ask for help when they're having a hard time. Kids can practice handling problems in a safe and controlled setting by playing roles.

This can boost their confidence and get them ready for real-life situations.

Setting up a helpful home environment

Kids should feel safe, loved, and understood at home in order to be supported. They can easily show how they feel, make mistakes without worrying about being judged, and learn from their mistakes. Here are some ideas for making your home a helpful place:

• Be clear about what you expect and how things will work out. Children need discipline and know what to expect. You give your child a sense of safety and stability by being clear about what you expect from them and always following through with the results.

• Help people talk to each other. Tell your child that they can talk about their feelings and thoughts without worrying about being judged or criticized. Tell them you'll always be there for them to talk to and listen.

• Enjoy both big and small wins. No matter how small the things your child does or attempts to do are, praise them. Giving your child lots of praise is a great way to improve their self-esteem and motivation.

• Show others how to communicate and solve problems in a good way. Kids learn by seeing what their parents do. You set a good example for your child to follow by communicating and fixing problems in a good way yourself.

You can give your child with ODD the confidence and strength to handle social situations and conflicts with others by helping them learn good communication and problem-solving skills in a safe and supportive home setting. Don't forget that change takes time. Don't give up if you don't see effects right away. Do not give up on your child; keep training, talking, and believing in their abilities. They can learn to deal with the problems that come with ODD and do well in all areas of their lives with your love and help.

Building a sense of connection and belonging

In the complicated dance of social interactions, everyone needs to feel like they fit and are connected. This is especially true for kids with Oppositional Defiant Disorder (ODD). These basic wants are like the roots of a tree; they keep the tree stable, feed it, and give it a solid base for healthy growth.

Fostering a sense of belonging and connection can be life-changing for kids with ODD, whose social interactions are often difficult. It can help them build grit, confidence, and a good sense of themselves. It's very important to make sure your child feels seen, heard, and valued. It's not enough to just meet their basic wants; you have to make an effort to connect with them on a deeper level.

This means giving them set time every day to do things they enjoy, listening to their thoughts and feelings without judging them, and recognizing what they're going through.

Always keep in mind that behind every child's bad behavior is a child who wants to be understood and accepted.

Family customs and rituals can be very effective at making people feel like they belong. Family dinners, game nights, or even simple bedtime habits can help kids with ODD feel like their lives are stable and predictable. These shared experiences bring people together, make them laugh, and connect with each other, forming a web of memories that strengthen family ties.

Encouraging your child to do things outside of school that are related to their hobbies can also help them feel like they belong. Whether it's a music group, a sports team, or an art class, these activities let you meet people who share your interests and help you make friends and improve your social skills in a safe space.

If your child is hesitant at first, gently push them to try new things, focusing on the fun and enjoyment of the action rather than the result.

Another important way to help your child feel like they fit is to praise their unique skills and strengths. Recognizing and appreciating each child's unique gifts can help them feel better about themselves and give them more confidence. Whether it's their artistic skill, athleticism, or intellectual interest, noticing and supporting their skills can help them feel seen and appreciated for who they are.

A feeling of belonging can also be built by making the home a place where people feel free to talk to each other and where differences are valued. This means actively listening, confirming feelings, and showing appreciation for each other's points of view. Going into a disagreement with empathy and understanding can help make it a safe place where everyone feels like they are being heard and valued.

Getting to know your child's teachers and other school staff well can also help them feel like they fit. You can show that you care about your child's education and well-being by staying in touch, going to parent-teacher conferences, and helping at school events. This way of working together can help build a network of support that makes your child feel like they fit at school and at home.

Remember that building a sense of connection and belonging is an ongoing process that needs love, patience, and understanding. There will be ups and downs, successes and failures, but if you work at it every day and care about your child's well-being, you can make your home a place where they feel loved, accepted, and able to handle the challenges of social relationships with strength and confidence.

Chapter 9: Role-Playing and Social Skills Training:

Using role-play to get better at talking to other people

You don't have to be an actor or improv fan to role-play. It's a powerful tool that can change how your child with ODD handles social settings. Imagine a place where your child can try out different social behaviors without fear of being judged. They can learn from their mistakes and eventually gain the confidence they need to do well in real-life situations. That is why role-playing is so fun!

How does it really work? Role-playing gives your child a chance to experience a social situation from someone else's point of view. You can make situations that are like real life ones, like asking a friend to play, joining a group talk, or figuring out a disagreement. By acting out these events, your child learns more about how people interact with each other, how to read body language, and how to talk to people   in   a   clear   way.

One of the best things about role-playing is that it lets your child make mistakes without worrying about what will happen in real life. They can try out different methods and new behaviors and find out what works best for them because they are free to do so.

With your help and advice, they can learn from their mistakes, improve their social skills, and eventually gain the   confidence   to   handle   social   situations   well.

You can also teach your child important social skills through role-playing, like how to actively listen, show understanding, and understand other points of view. Role-playing can help you show your child how to behave properly, talk to others, and get helpful feedback on how they're doing in social situations. Your child can learn these skills and use them in their daily lives by watching you do them and trying them in a safe place.

Another good thing about role-playing is that it can help your child learn how to solve problems and deal with conflicts. Your child can learn to find answers, negotiate with others, and find outcomes that are good for everyone by acting out situations where there are disagreements. This useful experience can give them the tools they need to handle disagreements well, with other kids and with adults.

Next, let's talk about some useful ways to use role-playing in your everyday life:

1. Pick situations that are true to your child's life: Pay attention to things your child does often or has trouble with, like getting along with friends, doing group activities, or handling being teased.

2. Make it fun and interesting. To make role-playing fun and interactive, use costumes, props, and silly sounds. Your child will learn more from the process if they enjoy it.

3. Give them support and positive feedback: Celebrate your child's wins, no matter how small, and focus on what they

do well. They will want to keep practicing and getting better at their social skills because of this good feedback.

4. Be gentle and understanding. Learning how to get along with other people takes time. Don't expect miracles to happen fast. Instead, focus on making small steps forward and enjoy each one.

5. Get help from a professional. If you don't know where to begin or need more help, you might want to talk to a therapist or social skills teacher who specializes in working with kids who have ODD.

The tools you use for role-playing can be changed to fit your child's specific wants and problems. By using role-playing as a parenting tool, you can give your child the social skills they need to handle friendships, fights, and everyday interactions with poise and confidence.

Don't forget that role-playing is only one part of the game. Using role-playing along with other methods for teaching social skills, like modeling, coaching, and positive feedback, can help your child grow and develop in the best way possible. Your child can get over their social problems and do well in all areas of life if you always back and help them.

Through our shared experience with Oppositional

efiant Disorder (ODD), we've learned a lot about the ups and downs of getting along with other people. We've talked about how role-playing can help you learn important skills. Now we'll talk about a method that works really well and is interesting: making social stories and plays.

Social scripts and stories are like personalized road maps that help you get through certain social settings. They break down conversations into steps that are easier for kids with ODD to handle. This helps them understand what is expected of them, guess what will happen, and learn how to respond appropriately. These resources will help your child feel more comfortable and ready to interact with others.

Making stories that stick with people

A social story is like a short story that is tailored to your child's specific events. It usually includes an account of what happened, who was involved, what should be done, and what could happen as a result. If your child has trouble sharing toys, for example, a social story might be about a playdate and stress how important it is to wait your turn and find ways to settle arguments.

Say this: "When I play with my friends, we sometimes both want the same toy." It's okay to be a little angry, but you should still share. We can each play with the toy for a while, or we can find something else to play with together.

Depending on your child's age and level of understanding, social stories can be as simple or complex as you need them to be. You can get them more interested by using drawings, pictures, or even real photos.

How to Have a Smooth Conversation

Social scripts are like social stories, but they focus more on interaction and talking. They teach your child specific words and movements to use in different social situations.

For example, if your kid has trouble starting conversations, a social script might give them some lines to try: "Hi, my name is [child's name]." Which one do you want?"

"Do you want to play with me?"

"Your shirt looks good on you." Where did you get it?"

Your child can feel less shy and more comfortable in social situations if they practice these lines ahead of time.

The Power of Making Things Unique

One great thing about social stories and plots is that they can be changed to fit different situations. You can change them to fit the interests and wants of your child. Include your child in the making process as much as possible; this will make them more invested and motivated.

If your kid really likes superheroes, you could write a social story about one who learns how to control their anger or share with their friends. If they really care about animals, you could write a script about them having to carefully ask for directions or wait in line at the zoo.

Adding Stories to Everyday Life

Don't just use social stories and plots for certain events. Use them in your daily talks and activities. You can read them out loud, play them out, or even make up your own versions. It's important for your child to use these tools as much as possible so they become natural to them.

Celebrating Little Wins

Don't forget that growth takes time and rest. Don't expect changes to happen quickly. Instead, praise even the smallest wins, like when your child uses a phrase from a social script or handles a tough social situation well. Giving people praise is a great way to boost their confidence and drive.

Making social stories and plays is a fun activity that you can do with your child that can help them handle social situations more easily and with more confidence. Your unflinching support and your child's amazing strength are shown by this. When you start this trip together, remember that each step forward is something to be happy about.

Using social skills training in everyday life: turning every interaction into a chance to learn

You've taken steps to help your child with ODD learn social skills and play pretend. They may have even started to understand the basics in organized settings.

The real magic happens when you use these skills with other people in real life. How can you practice your social skills without making it seem like you're not doing anything? Here's how to make your neighborhood and home a social skills lab:

1. Why the "teachable moment" is so powerful: Everyday events, no matter how big or small, are great chances to practice social skills. Did your kid talk over someone else? "Honey, I saw that you cut me off while I was talking to Grandma," you can say. Do you remember how we worked on waiting our turn?" Or maybe there was a fight with a brother. This is a chance to practice handling conflicts in a real-life setting. Teachable times are great because they happen without planning to. They're not planned and can be found anywhere.

2. Planning How to Interact with People Everyday: Daily activities offer a lot of opportunities to practice minor social skills. Family dinners can turn into lessons on how to have polite conversations by gently reminding everyone to listen, wait their turn, and show interest in others. Going to the grocery store can teach you how to be patient, wait in line, and talk to store workers in the right way. Even bedtime routines can be used to talk about feelings, show thanks, and make plans for socializing the next day.

3. Getting Social Skills Out of Playtime Summer camp: Children learn the most when they are playing. Support activities that naturally encourage working together, sharing, and talking. For example, making a fort together, playing board games, or participating in team sports are all great ways to learn how to get along with others. If you need to, don't be afraid to step in as a guide and offer gentle advice or good behavior as an example. Don't forget that kids learn best when they play!

4. Making connections in the community: making new

friends

Get your child to know people besides family and friends. Find things to do in the neighborhood that fit their interests. Whether it's a charity group, a sports league, or an art class, these places let you practice your social skills with people who like the same things you do. Remember that making friends takes work and time. Be kind, patient, and patient, and enjoy the little wins.

5. The Art of Positive Reinforcement: Reward your child when they do something good with other people. Did they wait in line at the ice cream shop for their turn? Thank them for their kindness. Did they say something nice about a friend? Thank them for being kind. Positive reinforcement works very well to make wanted behaviors stronger. When you notice and praise your child's social efforts, they are more likely to keep doing those good things.

6. Embrace the Mess: Mistakes Are Good for Learning: You don't learn social skills overnight. There will be problems, mistakes, and times when things don't go as planned. There's nothing wrong with this. Accept these "messy" times as chances to learn something. Talk to your child about what went wrong, come up with other ideas for how to fix it, and support them to try again. Remember that being resilient is a social skill in and of itself.

7. Work with teachers and therapists: it's very important to have a strong network of people you can talk to for help. Be honest with your child's teachers, therapists, and other workers who are helping to care for them. Talk about your

thoughts, problems, and achievements. You can make a regular and well-coordinated plan for improving social skills by working together.

Training in social skills should be a part of everyday life, not a goal that can be reached. It takes a lot of love, patience, and determination. However, the benefits are huge.

As your child gets better at these important skills, they'll feel better about themselves, make friends, and find it easier to interact with others.

Do not forget that you are not only showing them how to interact, but also giving them the tools they need to do well.

Chapter 10: Partnering with Professionals: The Role of Therapists, Counselors, and Teachers

Taking care of a kid who has Oppositional Defiant Disorder (ODD) can make you feel all kinds of emotions, from happiness to anger and everything in between. As a mom, you know your child better than anyone else. You don't have to go through this journey by yourself, though. A group of experts can help you and your child do well by giving you support, advice, and their professional knowledge.

Therapists are the builders of emotional health.

A lot of the time, therapists who specialize in ODD or child behavior problems are the ones who help kids understand and control their feelings. Think of them as architects who are making a plan for your mental health. Cognitive Behavioral Therapy (CBT) is one type of therapy that helps kids learn how to spot triggers, come up with ways to deal with problems, and question negative thought patterns.

For example, cognitive behavioral therapy (CBT) gives kids the tools to recognize and change the negative thoughts that make them act rebellious. Kids can change how they feel and act by learning new ways to think. Therapy can also help people improve their speaking skills, which can lead to better relationships with family and friends.

Think of therapy as a place where kids can talk about their feelings without worrying about being judged. They can learn how to express themselves in a healthy way, control their anger, and settle disagreements without violence in this safe place. Remember that treatment is not a quick fix. It is a process of learning about yourself and growing.

Counselors: The Key to Personal Growth

Counselors, who are often found in schools or community centers, help kids learn more about themselves and grow as people. They give kids a place to talk about their problems, worries, and hopes through one-on-one or group counseling meetings. Counselors can help kids learn how to get along with others, solve problems, and be strong when bad things happen.
Therapists can teach kids how to handle social problems in a healthy way by having them play different roles. They can lead chats in groups where kids can talk about their lives, learn from each other, and make friends who can help them. Counselors also speak up for kids with ODD and work with parents and teachers to make sure they are in a good setting where everyone feels welcome.

Think of counselors as trusted guides who give kids the tools they need to deal with problems, reach their full potential, and make real bonds with other people. Their advice can be especially helpful for kids who are having problems with their self-esteem or getting along with their peers.

Teachers: The People Who Help Students Do Well in School

Teachers are very important in a child's life, not just as teachers but also as role models and guides. They have the power to make the classroom a place where everyone feels welcome, engaged, and able to learn. A helpful and empathetic teacher can make all the difference for kids with ODD.

Teachers can use techniques to help students learn in the way that works best for them, deal with behavior problems, and encourage good social interactions. They can work with parents and teachers to make Individualized Education Programs (IEPs) that help students with specific problems do better in school.

Think of teachers as people who make learning possible. They teach and encourage a love of learning. Teachers can make sure that every child feels respected and able to do their best in the classroom by noticing and celebrating each child's unique skills and strengths.

How Working Together Can Help You

Most of the time, the best solutions happen when therapists, counselors, teachers, and parents work together. These experts can build a complete support system for a child that takes into account all areas of his or her life if they work together.

Sharing information and talking to each other on a regular basis is important to make sure that everyone is on the same page and working toward the same goals.

Don't forget that you're not on this trip by yourself.

Working with professionals can help you give your child the skills they need to get along with others, handle their feelings, and do well in school and in life in general. There may be hard times along the way, but your child can get through them and reach their full potential with your help.

How to Get Your Child the Help They Need

If you have a child with Oppositional Defiant Disorder (ODD), you probably know that you can't do it all by yourself. And you are totally right. Having a strong network of support is important for your child's growth and for your own health. Luckily, there are a lot of people who work full-time to help families just like yours. Take them as partners on this trip and work with them to give your child the skills they need to do well.

Your kid's "A-Team"

Imagine that your child has their own "A-Team" of professionals, each with their own set of skills that they can bring to the table. A therapist who specializes in working with kids who have ODD can give your child a safe place to talk about their feelings, learn healthy ways to deal with problems, and improve how they connect with others. Think of this therapist as your child's emotional coach who will help them learn more about themselves and learn how to control their emotions.

A therapist could be an important part of this team as well. Even though it's not always necessary, a psychiatrist can look at your child's mental health as a whole and tell you if medication along with treatment might help. Keep in mind that medication isn't a magic bullet, but it can help your child feel better by relieving some symptoms, which can make therapy and other treatments easier for them to do.

Different experts may join this group based on your child's age and specific needs. Your child can practice getting along with others in an organized and encouraging setting by joining a social skills group. An occupational therapist can help your child learn how to handle sensory information and focus better. They can also help them control their emotions.

How to Get Around in the Professional World

At first, it may seem impossible to find the right pros for your child, but don't give up. First, ask your family doctor or nurse for suggestions. A lot of the time, they can put you in touch with other reliable pros. You can also talk to your child's school; they might know of community tools and people who can help.

Trust your gut when you're interviewing possible therapists or psychiatrists. Find someone who is friendly, caring, and has worked with kids who have ODD before. Do not be afraid to ask them about how they work, how much they charge, and how much experience they have. You should look for someone who makes you and your child feel good and who you think can really help.

Remember that it may take some time and work to find the right people for your child, but it's worth it. Your child's life can change drastically if they get the right help. It can help them deal with problems, become more resilient, and learn the social and mental skills they need to do well.

Building a Partnership for Working Together

Once you've put together your child's "A-Team," it's important to work together with these pros. Tell them about your thoughts, worries, and plans. Be willing to listen to what they have to say. Always keep in mind that you are all trying to help your child do well.

As often as you can, go to therapy classes with your child. That way, you can better understand their problems, find new ways to help them, and grow closer to them during this process. Don't be afraid to ask the doctor questions or get more information. You can make your child's therapy a lot more successful by being involved in it.

Remember that your child's needs may change over time, so it's important to check in on their support system often. There's no need to be afraid to try something new if one therapist or solution isn't working. Being adaptable and aware of how your child's needs change is the most important   thing.
You can give your child the tools they need to deal with the challenges of ODD and reach their full potential by working with professionals and having a strong support system.

Don't forget that you're not going through this trip by yourself. Your child can do well and have a happy life if they get the help they need.

Working together with professionals to get the best results

Having an ODD (Oppositional Defiant Disorder) child is a unique journey that comes with its own set of challenges and successes. You are your child's strongest supporter, but it's important to know that you don't have to go through this alone. Putting together a team of professionals to help your child can make their life and the life of your whole family much better. This team-based method makes sure that your child gets complete, individualized care that is made to fit their needs.

The Power of a Team of Experts from Different Fields

Your child's care is like a puzzle; each expert adds a different piece to make a full picture of what they need. Therapists, psychiatrists, teachers, social workers, and other experts might be on a multidisciplinary team. Each professional brings something unique to the table and can give you a new way of looking at your child's problems and skills.

Therapists can help your child develop important coping and speaking skills by providing important emotional and behavioral support. Psychologists can check for and treat any underlying mental health problems in your child, making sure they get the right medicine if they do.

Teachers can make personalized lesson plans for your child that are based on how they learn best and what problems they are having. A social worker can help your family find community resources and support programs. These workers can make a treatment plan for your child that takes care of all of their health needs if they work together.

Building a Partnership for Working Together

It takes two to work together. You are an important part of your child's care team as a parent. Your thoughts, worries, and observations are very helpful. Don't be afraid to talk about your problems and ask questions. Don't forget that you know your child best. You must know and understand their specific personality and wants in order to work together effectively.

A good partnership is built on open conversation and respect for each other. Having regular talks with the people who care for your child can help make sure that everyone is on the same page. At these meetings, you can talk about success, voice concerns, and make any necessary changes to treatment plans. Remember that you both want the same thing: for your child to do well.

You can make a safe place for your child to feel understood, in control, and able to reach their full potential if you all work together.

Dealing with Problems and Enjoying Successes

There are hard times when you are a parent of a child with ODD. Along the way, there may be obstacles and anger.

But keep in mind that growth doesn't always happen in a straight line. Celebrate the little wins and big steps you've taken. No matter how small, each step forward shows how strong your child is and how much you support them.

Don't forget that you're not on this trip by yourself. There is a huge network of parents, professionals, and support groups that can help and inspire you. Don't be afraid to reach out and meet with people who know what you're going through. It can be very motivating to share your story and learn from others.

Accepting Hope and Strength

Even though having ODD can be hard, it's important to know that it's not a life sentence. Boys and girls with ODD can learn to handle their feelings, make friends, and reach their goals with the right help and support.

Working with professionals will not only help you give your child the best care possible, but it will also give them the skills and strength they need to do well.

The path may be long and twisting, but it is also full of hope and hope. Remember that you are the best person for your child. Your support, love, and patience are the most important things you have.

You can give your child a better future full of happiness, success, and satisfaction if you work with experts.

Conclusion - Recap of Key Takeaways and Strategies

You've learned about the complicated side of ODD and the ups and downs of friendships, arguments, and everyday exchanges. Let's boil down what we've learned to its most important parts before we end this help. Once again, it's time to think about those helpful methods and important lessons that will continue to guide you as a parent.

Remember that your child's ODD is not a sign of bad character. It has to do with the way the brain works and how the person experiences and interacts with the world. Your child's brain is set up to have strong emotional responses, which makes it harder for them to control their thoughts and impulses. We're not trying to blame or shame anyone. It's about getting to know your child, responding to their needs, and making a space where they can do well.

We've talked about tactics based on empathy, structure, and positive reinforcement all through this book. We've talked a lot about how important it is to communicate clearly, set reasonable goals, and have a strong bond with your child. We've talked about ways to handle social situations, settle disagreements, and make new friends.

As we wrap up, let's go over some of the most important points:

1. The Power of Connection: Your child will grow when they know you love and accept them. Spending valuable time with your child doing things they enjoy should be a

top priority. Don't forget that a strong mental bond can help you deal with the problems that come with ODD.

2. Clear and Consistent Communication: Kids with ODD do best when they know what to expect. Set clear rules and standards. If you need to, use simple language and pictures. Be steady with how you react to both good and bad behavior.

3. Positive reinforcement: Reward your child for their efforts and wins, no matter how small. Giving positive feedback can boost drive and self-esteem, which can lead to changes in behavior that are good.

4. Structure and routine: Giving your child a set plan every day can help them feel safe and calm down. Set regular times for things like meals, going to bed, doing homework, and doing jobs.

5. Training in social skills: Kids with ODD often have trouble getting along with other kids. Sign up your child for social skills classes or one-on-one counseling to help them learn how to make and keep friends.

6. How to Handle a Conflict: Teach your child healthy ways to handle disagreements, like pausing, speaking calmly, and asking an adult for help. Show others how to use these techniques, and do it with them in a safe place.

7. Take care of yourself: Being a parent of a child with

ODD can be hard on your emotions. Make sure that your health and happiness come first. Take breaks, talk to someone you trust or a doctor for help, and do things that make you happy.

Don't forget that this trip is a run, not a sprint. Sometimes progress is slow and lumpy, but don't give up. Your child can learn how to get along with others, handle disagreements, and make friends if you are patient, understanding, and give them the right tools.

Your constant help can make all the difference.

Let's not think about the problems too much as we come to an end. Let's instead praise your child's unique skills and abilities. It's clear that your kid is smart, artistic, and can do amazing things. Your child can get past the problems that come with ODD with your help and love. They will do well in every part of their life.

The road doesn't end here. It's the start of something new. Always be growing and learning, and always speak up for your child. Don't forget that you're not going through this trip by yourself. You and your family can do well with the help of many tools and support networks.

Parents are being told to enjoy small wins.

As a parent of a child with Oppositional Defiant Disorder (ODD), you will go through a long and hard process. The journey is hard, there are hurdles, and times when you may feel like you're moving back and forth between forward and backward. It's easy to lose sight of the progress you're making at this point. That's why it's important to enjoy every win, no matter how small.

Celebrating small wins doesn't mean you don't care about the problems. You should recognize the hard work you're putting in, the plans you're using, and the good changes you're seeing in your child. Your child is doing well when they can control their feelings, make their needs clear, or follow through with a request. It may not seem important, but these small wins are actually steps toward bigger goals and should be celebrated.

Celebrating small wins does more for you than just make you feel good. Studies have shown that noticing and praising even small accomplishments can have a big effect on our health and happiness. It can make us feel better about ourselves, encourage us to keep going, and make us stronger when bad things happen.

Parents of kids with ODD can have a more positive and hopeful view on life by celebrating small wins. This is especially important when dealing with the challenges of parenting a kid with behavior problems.

What can you do to celebrate small wins? Giving them a high-five, words of praise, or a special treat can be enough. You could make a "victory jar" and write down every little thing you've done well. You can look at it when you need to remember how far you've come.

Some parents use reward systems where kids can get points for good behavior that can then be exchanged for treats or benefits. The important thing is to find what works for you and your child and make it a habit to celebrate small wins.

Let's see what I mean. Imagine that your child, who often loses control when they're angry, is able to calm down in a tough situation. This is a big feat that should be recognized. Instead of dwelling on the fact that there was a frustrating scenario to begin with, praise their ability to handle their feelings in a healthy way.

Thank them for trying, let them know you see how far they've come, and encourage them to keep learning this skill. By celebrating this small win, you're teaching your child good behavior and giving them a sense of success.

Another example is when your child, who usually doesn't want to do what you say, does a job without complaining. This may seem like a small thing, but it's a big step toward working together more. Show your appreciation for their hard work and readiness to help, and maybe even give them a small reward as a thank-you. By enjoying this small win, you're getting your child to cooperate more and making things better between you and them.

Celebrating small wins isn't just a way to reward good behavior; it's also a way to change your focus. You're more likely to see your child's growth when you focus on the good things about their behavior, which can be very inspiring. It can also help you have a better relationship with your child, which is important for their growth and mental health.

When you have a child with ODD, remember that the trip is a marathon, not a sprint. Over and over again, things will go well and not so well. You can help your child have a more positive and hopeful view on life by celebrating the little wins along the way.

This will also boost their confidence, strength, and drive to keep trying. So, enjoy a moment of happiness today for a small win, no matter how small it seems. Because every little step forward is something to be happy about.

As this guide comes to a close, it's important to remember that your journey as a parent of a child with ODD is far from over. Understanding and handling ODD well is a journey that never ends, full of learning and growing. Information is one of the most useful things you can use as a parent. You can better help your child with ODD and deal with the specific problems that come up if you know more about it. Luckily, there are a lot of tools out there that can help, guide, and inform you further.

Books and other publications

There are a lot of informative books on ODD written by professionals in the field. You might want to read Ross Greene's "The Explosive Child." It gives you a compassionate way to understand and deal with difficult habits. "The ODD Workbook" by Sharon Saline is another great book. It is full of useful tips for parents. You can learn a lot of useful information and useful tips from these and other books that can really help you as a parent.

Groups and communities online that offer support

You're not the only one going through this. A lot of parents are raising kids with ODD, and staying in touch with them can save their lives. Support groups and online communities offer a secure area to talk about your feelings, ask questions, and get help.

These platforms can be very helpful for emotional support because they make people feel like they fit and are part of a group. It can be very comforting and energizing to hear from people who really understand what you're going through.

Therapy and help for people

Help from a professional can make all the difference in the world. Your child can learn how to deal with problems and handle their feelings by going to individual therapy. Family therapy can teach you how to talk to each other and solve problems in a healthy way. Don't be afraid to get help from a skilled counselor or therapist who specializes in ODD. They can provide personalized help and direction that can be very helpful in dealing with the difficulties of ODD.

Resources for Schools

It can be helpful to understand the science behind ODD. A lot of information about ODD can be found at sites like the Child Mind Institute and the American Academy of Child and Adolescent Psychiatry.

There are papers, webinars, and other resources that talk about what causes ODD, its symptoms, and treatments that have been shown to work. Getting educated is one of the most important things you can do to be a better supporter for your child.

Programs to teach parents

It takes special skills to be a parent of a child with ODD. Parent training programs, such as Parent-Child Interaction Therapy (PCIT) and Parent Management Training (PMT), can teach you how to deal with bad behavior and encourage good exchanges with your child. The goal of these programs is to give you the power to make your home a better place for relationships and harmony.

Groups that fight for causes

Families of people with ODD and other mental illnesses can get help from groups like CHADD (Children and Adults with Attention-Deficit/Hyperactivity Disorder) and NAMI (National Alliance on Mental Illness).

They give people tools, support, and a sense of belonging. Making connections with these groups can be a powerful way to get help, keep up with new studies, and speak up for your child's needs.

You are strong when you ask for help, not weak when you do not. Being honest about the problems and asking for help takes guts. You can get the information, skills, and help you need to deal with the challenges of ODD and give your child the tools they need to succeed by using the many resources out there.

Your journey goes on

Being a parent of a kid with ODD is a journey that never ends, but it's a journey full of hope and possibilities. Staying informed, connected, and supported can give you and your child the tools you need to face obstacles and make the future better.

Don't ever forget how powerful your love, kindness, and unwavering support can be.

You can help your child be confident and tough in the face of friendships, conflicts, and everyday encounters if you give them the right tools and advice.